THE
ELEMENTS
OF BECOMING
A SUCCESSFUL ASTROLOGER

EMILY KLINTWORTH

REDFeather™
MIND | BODY | SPIRIT

4880 Lower Valley Road, Atglen, PA 19310

Other REDFeather Mind, Body, Spirit Titles on Related Subjects:
Astrotherapy: Discover How to Live Better and Move Forward in Life with Your Astral Theme, Philippe Regnicoli, ISBN 978-0-7643-6074-9

The Beginner's Guide to Astrology: Class Is in Session, Dusty Bunker, ISBN 978-0-7643-5330-7

Traveling by the Stars: Have the Best Trip Possible Using Astrology!, Christine Rakela, ISBN 978-0-7643-6177-7

Designed by Jack Chappell
Cover design by Jack Chappell
Type set in Brandon Grotesque
Stock Image Credits: Photo by Christian Wiediger on Unsplash. Photo by Farzad Mohsenvand on Unsplash. Photo by Hafidh Satyanto on Unsplash. Photo by Maxim Tajer on Unsplash. Photo by Sachira Kawinda on Unsplash. Photo by Wesley Tingey on Unsplash. Shutterstock credit Maren Winter

ISBN: 978-0-7643-6629-1
Printed in India

Published by REDFeather Mind, Body, Spirit
An imprint of Schiffer Publishing, Ltd.
4880 Lower Valley Road
Atglen, PA 19310
Phone: (610) 593-1777; Fax: (610) 593-2002
Email: Info@redfeathermbs.com
Web: www.redfeathermbs.com

For our complete selection of fine books on this and related subjects, please visit our website at www.redfeathermbs.com. You may also write for a free catalog.

REDFeather Mind, Body, Spirit's titles are available at special discounts for bulk purchases for sales promotions or premiums. Special editions, including personalized covers, corporate imprints, and excerpts, can be created in large quantities for special needs. For more information, contact the publisher.

We are always looking for people to write books on new and related subjects. If you have an idea for a book, please contact us at proposals@schifferbooks.com.

Dedication

Many times on my path, I've been asked about God and how I bridge my faith and astrology. In these moments, I feel ever connected to God—

I feel the weight of my human body and the sacred vessel given to me. (God)

I look out around me and take in the trees purifying our air and the thought of rain nourishing the soil. (God)

I look up and see the sun providing warmth, stability, and the seasons. (God)

I look out at the person curious enough to ask a meaningful question to someone (me) who is different in their approach to life—seeking to build a connection. (God)

Last, I recognize God's persistence in all things and simply ask, "Who made the universe?"

Thank you, God, for my existence. Though I may never catch you in form, I know with all my being you exist. I hope you are happy and proud of your children on Earth. I hope that through our joys and sorrows we have found each other. I hope that you know you are loved so deeply and that I can hear you inside me and outside me.

I dedicate this book to you, God. The one who has been growing humanity since the beginning of time in an effort to bring new Spirits to heaven. You've been with me in my darkest moments and brought me back from depths my words could never describe. Thank you, God. Here's to the dawning of a new age. With your support and love, I hope to act as a midwife for the birth of many new, confident, service-oriented astrologers into the world.

CONTENTS

INTRODUCTION

Welcome! This book does not deal with memorization, interpretation technique, or how to understand the fundamentals. Instead, this book is meant to be a healing bridge as you learn to energetically step into this new role as astrologer successfully. I want to take you by the hand and guide you through the only way I can, honoring the elements and their creative power and teaching you to embody your role.

This book is divided into four sections: Fire, Earth, Air, and Water. Throughout the process, you will grow in confidence, create your first reading, develop a client-facing tool to help with readings, and set yourself up for success. You must do the work and not skip steps; everything is intentional in this book. I will train you, guide you, challenge you, develop you, and love you every step of the way.

We have a shared mission: to bring actual astrology to the world. This is our work, and I'm here to teach you how to make it yours, if that is your desire. I need more astrologers on this path with me. I need ones who are creative

> ❝ We are not competitors with each other.

healers looking to help others. I need the mystics and empaths. And I need the ones who don't fit into any current system, who have exciting talents they wish to merge with astrology. Let's pave the way together and usher in this new age.

We must say goodbye to the Age of Pisces. We are no longer playing the role of higher self to others, nor would we ever want to. We have no interest in the pursuit of world domination or power over the forces of nature. That energy served when it served, and we must powerfully sever the ties to it as we walk into what is needed now: self-empowerment, protection of sovereign consciousness, and supporting the true expression of the Soul.

This new age is about teaching people how to protect themselves, trust themselves, and get connected to God (in whatever way their soul desires).

I understand that there is much to learn beyond this book, and I am fully dedicated to your training. I have also created a simple Astrologer Training Program that works in conjunction with this book (Did you get it, in conjunction?). The program takes you through learning the signs, houses, planets, aspects, and more. This book is about helping you gain the confidence, create efficiently, and birth yourself into the world as an astrologer.

I am here if you need me, and I hope that my words support you on your path. Enjoy the experience. Do the work, and make this Taurus proud.

Your teacher,

Emily

PILLAR 1 OF THE CREATIVE PROCESS:

THE VISION (FIRE)

In this phase, you are in a state of inspiration. You experience a connection with the divine force, and you feel driven and motivated to expand and express. You love speed, and you don't ask questions, because the feeling is so intoxicating.

This energy courses through you and can create a feeling of being high. The longer you resist the energy of Pillar 2 (Grow It), the more at risk you are of accidentally dissolving the potency of your idea. You may even find yourself grasping tiny puzzle pieces, thinking you haven't figured out something yet.

1

DEAR NEW ASTROLOGER

Dear New Astrologer,

I'm so excited and grateful that you are here and reading these words. I love you.

We are the astrologers of the Aquarian Age.

We are the Indigo Children, rebels, underdogs.

We don't fit in, and we like it that way.

My role as a teacher is to provide you with all that you will need for this journey to become an official and professional astrologer. I will do everything I possibly can to support you in transitioning from a student of astrology to becoming a professional astrologer.

The result we seek: you confidently doing astrology readings as early as a week's time.

I want you to trust yourself and push yourself. I need you to be honest with yourself, open with yourself, and willing to propel yourself to your next level.

I was fortunate in my astrology journey to have extensive experience in training and development as a manager for Lush Fresh Handmade Cosmetics. I didn't realize it at the time, but my management experience is why I developed so fast and quickly as an astrologer.

At the moment of my writing this book, it has been nine years since I had my first astrology reading that sparked my desire to become an astrologer. In nine years, I have provided over a thousand readings, taught over a hundred workshops, worked as an astrologer at a premier well-being resort, published two books (this is now my third!), and read for a wide variety of clients, including a few celebrities. I currently teach for Uncommon Goods, run my business Absolutely Astrology, and I teach, train, and develop aspiring astrologers.

It's been a wild ride. But I've often asked myself, "How have I arrived here?"

It's one of those numerology things. The nine years preceding my astrology journey are how I made my astrology journey. I did what I knew to do, for better or for worse. I played the hand I had, not realizing that my approach was different from most other astrologers out there.

As I reflect, I think it came down to the fact that the moment I became a student of astrology, I immediately shifted into the role of the astrologer. I always believed I was a "New Astrologer." I was always both a student and a new astrologer at the same time. I still am.

I knew from my work in management that we're all new to the job when we first get hired. We are all inexperienced. We all have a learning curve. It was nothing unique to me, you know? In my mind, it was just the natural process of starting a new job. And I started the job (self-promoted, of course!).

I was not prepared, I had no real training, but I felt that the God force was on my side. That life would be my training and that I was the New Astrologer. Unexperienced and learning on the job.

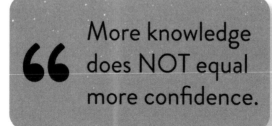

More knowledge does NOT equal more confidence.

If you are worried about progressions, transits, solar returns, natal planets . . . you have a massive customer service problem. No client can absorb that much information in a one-hour session.

Calculate it out. Most of my clients like to chat with me, which can take maybe 30 percent of the interaction. Another 20 percent is me explaining basic concepts. The remaining 50 percent is me offering my interpretation and asking them what it means for them (it's a dialogue between us).

I helped a woman gain the courage to sell her home simply because I explained the Jupiter transit, and that Jupiter was currently in her fourth house; she ran with that data! She put her house on the market, and it had multiple offers in less than twenty-four hours. She moved across the country.

It is that simple, but it does take absolute faith and trust in your clients.

I trust my clients. I trust them to be respectful, open, and responsible. I'm not open to anything less than that. Neither should you be.

> Trust me; you don't need to know EVERYTHING to know SOMETHING.

If you are reading this book, God has put the desire to read charts professionally in your heart. You may think it is insane and that there is no way that you can make it as an astrologer. I am here to tell you that you can.

You can incorporate these skills into your current professional role and excel right now. You can start reading charts intentionally and professionally as early as next week.

It has been my experience that there is a marketplace that is ready and eager to pay good astrologers for their excellent work. There are people right now wishing they could find a genuine, authentic, legitimate astrologer whom they can trust. Additionally, people are seeking new types of leaders within corporate structures. Long before I ran Absolutely Astrology, I was aligning my timing with the moon, including hiring fairs in my corporate gig and training my staff according to the moon (and I quickly discovered that this stuff works!).

There is a place for us in this world, but no one will show up at the doorstep and invite us. We must ask for ourselves.

So welcome. Welcome! Welcome! Welcome! I'm so grateful you are here.

You probably are wishing I would have been some mystical sage that showed up and told you that you had arrived with light beaming out of my heart at some profound moment in time, didn't you?

And yet, here it is.

You are the mystic sage who found this book. I am the relentless, stubborn Taurus who will never stop until

I empower all astrology students to make this leap and embody their professional astrologers hidden inside.

Here is my wish.

I wish you to be a brilliant and balanced astrologer now. You might be inexperienced and new to the job, but as far as I'm concerned—you're hired! Take the job. Please know that you are not exiting your path for another. Please understand that it's astrology + all the skills you already have. It's the combo platter. Take astrology and apply it to what you are doing. If you work in the corporate world, add it into who you are, how you move, how you decide, and how you lead. Combine it all. You are an astrologer + all the other things.

I'm a trainer and an astrologer. Through my corporate gig, the training was learned and has served me very well in developing workshops, teaching lectures, providing readings, and developing astrologers. The trainer in me didn't end when I embodied the astrologer inside me. She was a part of the whole process.

So your first step is for you to answer this question from your inner truth: "Do you accept this job as an astrologer?"

> Combine astrology with your current skill set. "

If it isn't a 150 percent yes, I can't help you. Without commitment, you will burn out in the earth stage of manifestation. It has to be an absolute yes. And you have to be willing to be the newbie.

All right, it's time to commence your training!

THE CREATIVE PROCESS USING THE FOUR ELEMENTS

Let's get started. It's time to prepare the seedling, set the course, and determine the direction of your sun.

Astrology directly shows us the creative process through the elements: Fire, Earth, Air, and Water. The creative process repeats over and over and over again. Whenever you create, you will move through this process, whether you are writing a new book, building a new house, entering a new relationship, or starting a new career. It is a creative process—all of it, and it flows precisely like the elements.

The creative elemental pillars look something like this:

Pillar 1: Fire	Creation Mode, Inspiration, Speed, Ideas, Awakening
Pillar 2: Earth	Organization, Planning, Persistence, Prepare
Pillar 3: Air	Problem-Solve, Elevate, Strategize, Pivot, Change
Pillar 4: Water	Purpose, Meaning, Reflect, Connect, Flow, Alignment

As far as I know, we all work with the creative process precisely the same. We move from Fire to Earth, to Air, to Water. The astrological elements are the creative process. God created the zodiac (archetypes of our consciousness) through the elements, and we also create through the elements.

The better you focus your energy at each particular stage of the creative process, the more you will pull from that stage. This is what I often call the "slinky effect." A slinky can be squished, and you can gain little momentum from a single ring, or it can be stretched, and you will gain massive momentum from a single ring. The more you stretch and understand each stage, the more power you draw from the creative process.

This book, which aims to coach, train, and develop you into the energy of the professional astrologer, is based and rooted in astrology (the elemental mechanics). This has been the most profound way I have worked with astrology in my endeavors, by genuinely understanding its foundations and applying it to my life. The focus is NOT to have you memorize more keywords, but to get you out of that linear process, learning a bit of astrology at a time and then immediately sharing it.

Most of us will favor certain stages of the creative process (and thus, we can get stuck there). For instance, if someone is dominant Earth in their natal chart, they will probably value the activities of the Earth phase: manifestation. The place of *doing*. And they will likely resist Air and the need to elevate and strategize. In other words, they get stuck doing the same things repeatedly, making little progress because they can't strategize or pivot as needed to accelerate their growth.

On the other hand, if someone is all about the Fire phase, they will enjoy the process of visualizing and intention setting and place a high value on this. They want the speed, downloads, and uploads and will feel very satisfied playing with ideas. They will often resist the Earth element and the stage of *doing*.

I have found a high correlation between the dominant element of a natal chart and how one works through the creative process. You can learn more about your strongest element in my workbook, *Claiming Your Power through Astrology*.

Keep in mind that this is the typical pattern of resistance I have seen over and over again:

> Fire resisting Earth
> Earth resisting Air
> Air resisting Water
> Water resisting Fire

This book is divided into four sections for each of the elements. You are currently in chapter 2 of the Fire section, and we are consciously working on the energy, visualization, downloads, and uploads around this journey you are embarking on. We need all the stages, and our goal is to get as much out of each stage as possible.

There is a moment on your path where this seedling desire to become the astrologer was planted in your heart. It is the activation of the Fire pillar of the creative process. It has probably happened to you in many ways throughout your path, not just with astrology. Perhaps you experienced this fire activation around: wanting to get in shape, wanting to have kids, wanting to get married, wanting a new job, wanting to travel, and now wanting to be an astrologer.

The creative process always starts in the Fire stage. It's an activation from God/Source/Universe. It's something I believe you can NOT conjure up but instead is placed in you from the divine to sustain you and support you as you grow. Occasionally, if you're stubborn like me, the seed attempts to make its way to you multiple times. Here is how it looked on my path.

The first attempt to deliver that "astrologer seed" happened when I was on a trip to California in elementary school, visiting my friend's aunt. The aunt was an actual astrologer and actively tried to share astrology with us. I had no interest at the time. I deflected and didn't receive the call.

At twenty-seven, I moved into an old fixer-upper bungalow, and the previous owner left many books behind. In the closet, I discovered an old dusty set of encyclopedia books and one astrology book. I was mildly interested but too busy at work to begin to study. I put the text on the shelf for years. I deflected, but this time I held on to it like it might be an option.

On the third attempt, my sister purchased an astrology reading for me for my thirtieth birthday. In the reading, the astrologer asked if I was a published author. I had ALWAYS wanted to be an author, and the fact that the chart saw that blew my mind. I finally accepted that seed; I officially wanted to be an astrologer because I desired to do what she did: see the soul's truth.

Recognizing the seedling moment is essential, but it is equally important to acknowledge the attempts that didn't land. By doing so, you see that there is a more significant pattern and that what you feel in your heart belongs to the force of God.

I want you to write out your seedling moments and your point of activation. Within every single seedling exists an etheric blueprint that is a flexible and evolving plan to achieve the desire. By bringing your attention to *why* you want to be an astrologer and how your desire was planted, you will accept the etheric blueprint and receive an activation.

I find that in the Fire stages of creation, people are obsessed with getting a full download or a whole version of the plan with step-by-step instructions on how everything will fall into place. You don't get to see all that. The journey you are taking is in your heart, not your mind.

> Know this:
> You do not
> need to
> understand
> the blueprint.

The plan is living. It needs to be.

We aren't perfect, and this etheric blueprint must be able to self-correct as we go along our paths. A step-by-step linear download is not possible when you are embarking on a multidimensional leap. It's a flexible and evolving journey *on purpose*.

Let's take ownership of this seedling together so that you are directly connected to the etheric blueprint.

MEDITATION

STEP 1:

TRAVEL BACK IN TIME

Take about five minutes to clear your mind and travel to the moment in time where you felt the seedling inside you activate. Visualize yourself outside your physical body, watching yourself go through the motions. See if you can connect with yourself and get the attention of the ego. If you can, ask to see the seedling in the heart. If you cannot, simply focus on your body.

STEP 2:

HOLD THE VISION

I want you to pretend that you are looking through a telescope that will narrow in on the seedling. Look at yourself and focus on your heart and imagine the seedling there. Use the telescope to move past the physical body and examine it. Look to see what color the seed is, the size, and if it has yet sprouted. Talk to the seedling and share your gratitude for its support. Within this little seedling is energy so profound that words cannot explain.

Connect with the seedling. Do not move it. Do not touch it. Let it be in your heart at that moment. Pay witness.

STEP 3:

FEEL IT NOW

Take your left hand and open your palm, touching it to your heart. Find the same seedling in your heart right now and speak to it. Feel it. Love it. Be with it.

You may ask it questions and tell it "Thank you." Be sure not to overwhelm the energy by demanding things; simply allow it to support you and love you back.

I have found that the most profound energy work is simple and easy to do. Whenever you feel you need to connect with this energy, put your left hand to your heart. This is an anchoring exercise that brings you to the moment you were sent on this path. It holds infinite energy to support you.

ASTROLOGY VS. THE ASTROLOGER

(DROP THE PRESSURE!)

Okay, we need to get two energetics crystal clear in your consciousness right now. Two things you need to know right off the bat for this new gig you have as an astrologer:

1: Astrology belongs to God / Spirit / the Universe. The cosmos is doing all the work, and everything that happens is 150 percent credited to the *force*.

2: You're the astrologer. You help other people understand, work with, and gain awareness from the hard work of astrology.

If these two things sink in, you will know that we as the astrologers do not do the "heavy lifting." We do not have anything to do with the accuracy, power, and absurdly superior *force* in motion through the cosmic energies. We are independent from its power. It exists with or without us.

Those who manipulate, exploit, or try to defile astrology are not in a good place energetically. It is my personal belief that if you mistake your power and entangle it with the power inherent to astrology, you will have a massive ego trip. I warn you, don't go in that direction.

Early on, the only transit I wanted to work deeply with was the Saturn transit. I had read *Astrology for the Millions*, and I was *in love* with all of it. I still am.

I would explain the whole transit and walk people through it, providing dates. I would say things like, "Hey, this is when Saturn entered your fourth house in the year 1982. It can represent a new fresh start of a journey. Can you remember anything significant?"

Most of the time, they would be like, "Yes! That's the year I got promoted, and we moved across the country. Oh yeah! And then we had a baby!"

I was practicing being an interpreter. I wanted to leave it open ended so that I could learn and they could learn too. Once I heard the same thing multiple times, I would update my reading process, and then I would say something like, "When Saturn enters the fourth house, it is common for people to move or begin a new phase in their career, get married, or have a baby. It is a time of starting a new journey. Can you remember anything significant from the year 1995?"

I want you to notice that all I have ever done is add more to my translation of astrology.

At first, it is just one little tidbit. Then I share it, and I get more confirmation of accuracy or inaccuracy. If I shared that Mars in the second house could mean you are not responsible with money, and ten people told me that doesn't add up since they are great with money, I would alter my interpretation. I never fought the data, and I trusted that my interpretations pertaining to my clients (the ones God brings to me) were where I needed to focus. Does that make sense?

I don't emotionally feel responsible for Mars in the second house. I just feel responsible for what I've learned when I sit down and share with my clients. I can imagine most people might feel a bit embarrassed if they said, "Mars in the second means you're bad with money." And someone was like, "Not at all. I'm a billionaire, and that is completely *wrong*."

I would feel bad if I said that too. I don't mind the response because it feels like a match!

I say things differently, and thus the response I get is entirely different. In the early days, you would have heard me say something more like this:

"Now we have Mars, which is the planet of action and masculine energy. It is the point where you feel inspired to take action. It can, at times, be impulsive. You have it here in the second house, connected to finances, resources, and money. Do you find that you struggle with overspending at times? Or perhaps does the money come to you sporadically in mighty bursts and then withdraw?"

In this case, if it is an inaccurate interpretation, I haven't offended my client or made them upset by presenting a bold statement out of nowhere. I like to explain my interpretations; it takes away the "personal" and allows it all to breathe.

To be sure, I do find that Mars in the second house does often express as an impulsive and active spender, and Venus does typically mean there is no need to worry about finances in this life. I have the confidence to say this because I gathered data along the way and preface it by saying things like, "typically means" or "often expresses."

At this point, I'm hoping that you are fully recognizing and permitting yourself to be in the stage you are at. I am equally hoping you understand that you are just as powerful now as you will be ten years from now. I can't say who met me at a "better time" on my path as an astrologer . . . was it the person who met me in person in the early days, when I was very slow and steady, working just one section of a chart? Or is it the person who meets me virtually today when I am bouncing off three charts simultaneously? My level of service is precisely the same. My energy and intention have not shifted one bit from day one until today.

It takes a deep and active *faith* in the God force to know that the right people come at the right time. It is always happening in the right way at the right timing. The person who needed me only to teach the Saturn transit arrived on time. The person who needed me to look at past-life connections to their ex also came on time. My job? To show up and do each reading better than the one before it.

We are in the Fire stage of this book, and I am energetically preparing your mind to move forward with deep congruence. If you show up in a first reading thinking you are supposed to be some magical guru with all the answers, you will fail. But why will you fail?

Because we aren't magical gurus, and we never will be. Take a deep inhale and exhale. Release the pressure. We interpret and empower our clients, and astrology does the "astrology."

Right now, I want you to start paying attention to how I word things. See if this feels right to you. You have my blessing to adopt this language for sharing and use it as yours. If you want to expand and write out your own, you may do that as well.

Please read, work with, absorb, attune, and take on this way of approaching your interpretations, using these sentences:

> "I'm just getting started learning this fascinating language, and I'm so grateful I get this opportunity to share with you."

"I'm still a bit new at this, but what I see here is that there is an alignment between these two planets. Here is what it might mean . . . what does it mean to you?"

"I learned this new cool technique that explores your career development. Would you be willing to sit with me and look at the dates to see if it resonates?"

"I've been fascinated with astrology and have often found it to be very accurate. Would you be open to hearing more and sharing with me whether it resonates or not?"

"Yes, this can happen that the chart does not line up. Astrology is a tool for self-development and supporting us in expanding the way we think; it's an art, and not everything will always pertain to your situation. Let's let that piece go and look at another part of the chart."

"That's interesting; you don't find yourself extroverted, but the chart indicates this. Hmmm. Just out of curiosity, how do you think your friends and family would describe you?"

"Yes, I do see that there is a lot of energy around stepping into motherhood in your chart, and that would seem strange that you haven't had kids. I don't think this means anything has gone wrong in any way. I have found that the motherhood desire can be archetypal. Have you found that you naturally take on a mothering role to those at work or with close friends? Do you have any pets?"

As you can see, we are NEVER pushing against our clients. There is no point! We are there to serve them and help them move forward. Astrology is our tool, but it is only one of many tools we have. For instance, self-compassion and empathy are just as powerful.

On two separate occasions, I have read for mothers whose children committed suicide. I know how strange that might sound, but it has happened. I felt like I had nothing to offer, and I couldn't understand why God had brought them to me. Instead of shrinking back in fear, I opened my heart and asked questions, and I listened. I made choices rooted in compassion, and did all that I knew to do, hoping that it might be of comfort somehow.

I have found myself reading charts for no other reason than just the mere fact that, in so doing, it would allow a mother to feel closer to the child again in a way that promoted healing. We will do some things that we will feel ill prepared for astrologically, but with compassion as our root, we will be led by God to share as we are meant to.

MORE KNOWLEDGE DOES NOT EQUAL MORE CONFIDENCE

I don't care how many books you have read or facts you have memorized. At a certain point, you will hit a learning ceiling. The mind needs to apply this knowledge in real-life situations to improve.

Your job is to show up and read every time better than the time before it. It's a simple expectation, but one you can manage. If you follow it and extend yourself out of your

> Knowledge is knowledge. Wisdom is wisdom. "

comfort zone, you'll grow deliberately.

You have to share what you can, chart by chart. Eventually, you become fluent and confident.

It's like learning a foreign language through immersion. You put yourself in the energy and the space at the start. You don't lie about being new, but you're "there" being "new."

The only reason I can sit down and read a chart without hesitation isn't magic. I struggled. It took me a week to memorize the order of the zodiac. I drew mental images in my mind like a map. Then I showed up and made offers to read for people. It's because I read chart after chart after chart that I become fluent. In my opinion, you won't be fluent until you get out there and do the thing you want to become fluent in.

This often scares people. Questions of not being worthy and not knowing enough. Of being a fraud. But how can you be a fraud if you tell the person you're new and excited to share what you've learned so far?

As long as you are honest, you will have no problems. Stay away from financial and legal advice. Focus on helping people understand themselves. Most people on Earth get literally no help on how to develop their connection to their souls, and astrology is a direct link. The fact that we readily signed up for the job? It makes most people incredibly grateful.

I used to say things like,

> "I'm learning about these things called astrological houses. Most people don't know about them. Have you heard about them?"

> "Hey, did you know there are two zodiacs? This one I use is based on the seasons and is called the Tropical Zodiac."

> "You know, this planetary alignment could be interpreted in multiple ways, and I'm still a bit new at this. I see the sun as representing self-expression in this life. I see it here in House 9. Read these words that are connected to the ninth. Is there a message in this for you?"

I would give simple advice:

> "You might want to read your horoscope for a rising sign and your sun sign. It will give you better information that way."

> "The moon sign you're born under is connected to your past lives. Do you believe in reincarnation? You should explore this moon sign in depth to learn more after the session."

As always, it isn't what you say but how you say it. One of the hidden gifts inside our role as astrologers is to pose the right question to the right person at the right time. To stimulate them to think differently so that they may perceive differently. That perception will lead to new ways that they act in the world, and often shifts them spiritually.

One single question posed to me in an astrology reading changed my life. Here is what you need to keep in mind: it wasn't a "huge thing" for the astrologer to say. It didn't require some crazy advanced technique hidden away from the public and saved only for the astrological elite within some mystical circle. It was the simple observation of the ninth and third house within my natal chart and a simple question to match: "I'm curious, Emily; are you a published author?"

Right now, I need you to start to realize that you're ready now. You get to work with the knowledge you have now. And don't fool yourself into thinking you can't.

Let me show you what I mean . . . let's say you know only the zodiac, but you know it backward and forward. You could do sessions that taught people about all the meaningful relationships in their lives and the differences between the signs. You could sit with a mom of four children and take her on a sacred journey of understanding her children. You could draw a zodiac and place each child inside the zodiac. Can you see how genuine sharing shapes the entire experience? I don't think a mom out there wouldn't appreciate that perspective and attention to detail.

When you bring sacred energy to astrology, you transform everything. Be that person. As I've grown, my clients have changed to meet me at my skill set. Think about it. I served people who NEVER worked with astrology or considered it at the beginning. As I learned more, God brought me different people at the right time to nurture and stimulate my development (and theirs).

Today, I help a variety of people. It may look different on the surface, but I serve from this same energy of showing up, sharing what I've learned, and aiming to grow every single time. And guess what? I always get the same feedback, "I love the way you explain things."

There is a very destructive thought in the collective psyche that says that to provide a good service, you have to know everything. Not true. Excellent customer service is born from the exact opposite awareness. It's accepting that you can't know everything, and you must provide a dedicated service that accounts for that. It means constantly being willing to grow and create a relationship based on trust with your clients.

I can tell you point blank: it's not the amount of information you have, but how you treat people and the way you share it. When we are nurturing the Fire stages within the creation process, you must steady your expectations. There is a difference between trying to share information about the zodiac versus trying to read progressions. And by the way, I do not read progressions! Right now, I need you to pick an area within astrology that's going to be your initial starting place (mine was career through the Saturn transit). Just select one thing that you will expand on, grow, share, and create momentum through. If you attack all the astrology at one time, you'll spin yourself round in circles. You won't be setting yourself up for success, because Rome wasn't built in a day. Here are some ideas to get you started. Please feel the energy in your body and see what calls to you, inspires you, and excites you. Astrology can look at various parts of your life, and you can pick a speciality. For instance, there is vocational astrology for the career you are best

Be where you're at and own it.

> **Brick by brick.
> Chart by chart.**

suited for. Travel astrology includes sacred places to visit or where to live for success. Relationship astrology helps understand the dynamics between two souls. There is electional astrology for timing events. And then within these wider categories, you can narrow things down even more and practice a technique. For instance, Venus in the natal chart can show where you are most likely to find monetary success. Saturn in the natal chart can show the cycles of your career growth.

Once you have your starting point, you need to change how you study to flood your system and build an experience around your area of expertise. Remember, once you start sharing it, it will eventually become second nature. You'll do ten readings on just the zodiac for relationships, and suddenly you'll get a nudge from Spirit. It will be time to incorporate another thing.

Most new astrologers run the risk of getting stuck in a "student mentality," and this is a trick because, more than likely, it isn't more knowledge they need but practice. When you practice sharing the data, you commit those pieces into muscle memory. You begin to build a solid foundation, and as you learn new "tricks" along the way, you simply add them into the mix. Much anxiety develops if you do not learn and practice equally.

Please know, you're not in competition with anyone but who you were yesterday. You cannot measure your success by comparing yourself to others; it's irrelevant. Measure yourself on the basis of who you were yesterday. Your progress is up to you and is ultimately your responsibility.

As you embark on this journey, you'll keep blending and adding in the basics. Through this process, God will reveal to you which direction to go in. You'll discover what lights up your soul, and you'll follow it.

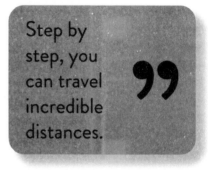

Step by step, you can travel incredible distances.

You might decide to expand your specialty to travel or vocation. You might love reading charts for teenagers. Heck, you might read the chart of pets! The thing is, no one can unlock this secret but you. And as far as I know, God grants you this awareness when it's the right time.

Right now? You pick your starting place. Your first move. What's it going to be? You don't have to pick off my list. You could serve only Scorpios and master the deacons on levels no one has ever done before! You can do it any way you want. But you must pick a strong, sturdy, realistic place to start.

If you're feeling inspired, email me and tell me your starting place, because I'd love that! There is power in the written word, and I know this firsthand. You can email me your starting place to emily@absolutelyastrology. com. I'm dedicated to training you and creating the structure you need to succeed. If you show up, I'll show up. I promise.

PILLAR 2 OF THE CREATIVE PROCESS:

SELF-ORGANIZATION (EARTH)

In this phase, you are in a state of cultivation. You are ready to do the hard work and show up. You set yourself to the course, and you keep putting one foot in front of the other. You are determined and persistent in your quest.

This energy courses through you and makes you feel unstoppable and unbreakable. The longer you resist the energy of a pillar, the more at risk you are for putting in the hours without any results. You may even find yourself trying to work harder and harder, and the results becoming more elusive in the process.

5

A READING VS.
AN EXPERIENCE

You might be thinking that this is all fine and dandy, but how do you actually apply it? What will you actually be saying and doing? Great question! That is what we will address right now as we officially enter into the Earth pillar of the creative process.

Up until now, we have been working primarily with ideas and thought forms. We've created awareness around you accepting the job as the astrologer, shifting your perception around what an astrologer does, claiming your initial starting point, and ultimately learning that you are ready now.

It's time to take the energy work of the inner world and make it physical. That's why I'm now going to walk you through creating your first signature experience. [Loud applause] You're going to hone in on your skill set and develop a solid outline for what you will cover in your initial astrology sessions.

When it comes to sharing, the more connected you are to the service you provide, the more you will naturally attract your ideal clients at every stage of your growth. I always have and will always work off outlines. I fine-tune my outlines until they serve my clients and me equally, and there is a feeling deep down in my soul of completion, arrival, and connection.

> This is what Earth energy is about, building structures and containers that actively support development. "

> **66** We create outlines for consistency in our customer service.

Consistency is vital in providing sensational customer service and development. Think about it: Let's say you give a fantastic session to Suzy. Suzy becomes pumped and talks you up to her friend Liz. She tells Liz everything you did in your session. Liz signs up and is excited for weeks! She wants the same experience you gave to Suzy. Liz shows up, and she gets something entirely different. She's angry and disappointed, and she tells Suzy. Obviously, if this were to happen, that would suck, and it could potentially lose your clients.

In an ideal world, you always provide a consistent experience. This way, when Suzy recommends your session to Liz, it will be warmly and wholeheartedly received by Liz! Your consistency ensures that Liz gets what Suzy recommended to her.

There have been plenty of people in this world who have gone to an astrologer and walked out not understanding a word they said! I know this because they tell me about it! The trouble is, if you just read a chart and don't involve your client, you are going to fall short. You need excellence in customer service and to provide an experience, not just a reading.

A reading versus an experience is the difference between being linear and going through the motions on autopilot versus being completely present and multidimensional. If you ever see glossed-over eyes, distracted clients, or no-repeat clientele, you lack the multidimensional presence within your services. It is an easy mistake to make, and I'm sure we have all made it. Don't personalize it, but rather learn from it. Adapt. Change. Move on.

For me, when I see some things not working in a session, I just change. I do not typically abandon outlines, but I make necessary "tweaks" as I go. The goal is to serve my clients, and if something within my outline doesn't work, I'm not hanging on to it. I don't think I am bad or I've done something wrong when a technique or approach doesn't work as intended. I recognize that the actual process is in the revision (something I learned through studying creative writing).

Please know, I'm not suggesting you turn into a robot (that's what happens in linear readings that don't actually engage clients). I am also not recommending you have a memorized script that you read without personality. I'm recommending that you have a robust and fluid outline that is tested and works 80 percent of the time.

If you have completed my astrology workbooks, you can see the early outlines I have used in my live readings. *Claiming Your Power* is based on my outline for natal chart readings. *Your Cosmic Compass* is based on the outline I use for my solar return chart sessions.

You have my blessing to work off my outlines from those books as a starting point, but you still need to follow the process below. Use it as a point of inspiration, but recognize that you have your own unique and beautiful way of working with astrology. I want as much of you and your skill set as possible in this outline.

Okay, let's get started and build an outline together!

YOUR FIRST ASTROLOGY EXPERIENCE

CREATING THE OUTLINE

Getting Started: The Earth pillar is about making things manifest; transforming thought into its next evolution. For many, this is how writing serves as the first anchor to thought. It is not the Earth pillar if you can't see, taste, touch, and feel it.

Prepare a single piece of paper:

Step 1: Grab a piece of paper and fold it in half vertically to create a strong crease.

Step 2: Now, turn it landscape and draw a line over the crease on the front and back.

Step 3: You will have four sections. Number them 1–4, the first two sections on the front page, and the last two sections on the back.

Step 4: Follow my directions below and physically write your answers on this prepared piece of paper.

SECTION 1:

INTRODUCTION

This material will cover the first five to ten minutes of a sixty-minute session.

In this section, you will write out and develop the first ten minutes of your reading. Our internal intention within the first five to ten minutes of the session is to figure out how we can best serve the client. We do this by bringing them into our world and asking appropriate questions relevant to our particular process. We must make this process engaging, inspiring, and authentic. You cannot just blandly ask questions, or you will not build an authentic connection.

You do not want to rush or drag this section out. Watch for key indicators in your client to determine their level of engagement with this part of the process. Answer the questions below to anchor in what you will be doing to ease your client into your reading and to get them excited about the experience.

Please handwrite the question and your answer to it onto the first segment of your paper, marked "1."

Question 1: In one sentence, what is the key takeaway you will give through the experience?

That is, how elements work, and to provide three critical insights about their chosen relationship.

Question 2: What will you call this session?

For example, Elemental Astrology Session.

Question 3: How will you be able to build trust and connection at the beginning of your session?

Such as, meditation, story, overview, example, mention a current astrological event, etc. For instance, the mediation might be to activate the Fire/Earth/Air/Water element, or the story might be about realizing a deficient element and learning how to remedy it.

Questions 4: What are three questions you can ask to help get to know your client better and to help you customize later portions of your session?

For instance, are there any relationships you desire to understand better? That is, are there any conflicts in a relationship you would like to explore from the past or in the present? (i.e., Would you be open to exploring your relationship with yourself during this session, or would you instead rather focus on external relationships?).

SECTION 2:

DELIVER AND ENGAGE

This material will cover the next twenty minutes of a sixty-minute session.

The next twenty minutes is where you deliver the first round of your astrological interpretation. It is natural for the astrologer to speak more during this segment of the experience, and this is okay because it allows the client to fully understand the process. Be detailed and watch body language to know if you need to slow down or speed up. You must have a rhythm and a way of moving through your information, so it has the right speed (this can be learned only by practicing). Answer the questions below to help you shape this segment of your reading. Please write both the question and answer into the next segment on your paper, labeled "2."

Question 1: What astrological principle would you be able to explain easily for this particular session?

For example, astrological elements: Fire, Earth, Air, Water.

Question 2: Can you quickly explain the concept from the last question in two paragraphs? Try it now.

For instance, the zodiac was created on the basis of elemental energies that we are all intimately connected to: Fire, Earth, Air, and Water. Each element has natural tendencies. For instance, Fire is considered bold/ active, Earth is considered grounded/resourceful, Air is elevating/far-reaching, and Water is caring/ nourishing.

Two of the elements harmonize in the zodiac, and two elements don't. Imagine putting Earth on Fire, and you will see this in nature (Earth will smother Fire). Air and Fire are harmonic, as are Earth and Water. Through the Sun sign, you can often see that these elements either gravitate to or away from each other. All elements can get along, and learning about the elements will support you in bringing more awareness into your relationships. We will be exploring your most-important relationships today.

Question 3: How do you plan to move through your interpretations?

For instance, in the session we will move through the elements and teach the basics. I will have the client bring to the session a list of five essential people currently in their life, along with the birthdates for each. We will look at the Sun sign only. Once I explain the element, I will see who on their list is of that element. We will note large patterns through this process. For example, is the client attracting a dominant element? Is there a whole element missing?

Question 4: What exact process will you follow?

As an example, I will start with Fire and give a one-minute summary. I will then share the Fire signs of Aries, Leo, and Sagittarius. We will identify the Fire element on the "important relationships" list that I will empower the client to bring to the session. Once the Sun signs of Fire are placed, I will ask if this information fits, and listen to my client's perspective. We will do the same for Earth, Air, and Water.

PROMPTS FOR SECTION 3

This material will cover the next twenty minutes of a sixty-minute session.

The intention at this point is to reestablish the connection you created at the beginning of the session. It is where you check back in and make sure the client's needs are being met. You will then move deeper into the information presented, working to apply the knowledge. The dynamic of speaking should be close to equal between the astrologer and client at this phase, and this happens when the delivery is relevant and understandable. Please answer the questions below on your outline labeled as section 3.

Question 1: How can you go deeper and add more meaning to the steps you took in the last section?

For example, in the last segment, I would have a circle that is divided into the four elements, where I entered the important people by element. I could now teach about harmonics and use a green and a red marker to draw lines between the important relationships.

Question 2: How can you help the client solve, understand, or apply what you have taught?

For instance, once I draw in the lines, I can provide tips on how uncomplementary elements can learn to communicate better with each other. For instance, I can explain that the Fire element will gain much by slowing down and listening more when around Earth and Water.

PROMPTS FOR SECTION 4

This material will cover the final ten minutes of a sixty-minute session.

The intention for the last ten minutes of a session is to bring closure and completion to the material covered. It's hoped that by the end of your session, you will have created a powerful connection with your client. You not only have demonstrated your skill set but also have taken the time to ensure that you were providing a well-rounded experience. Answer the questions below to complete your outline and finish the section labeled "4."

Question 1: How will you ensure the customer feels complete?

For example, I will provide ten minutes at the end for questions and summarize the main points. I will verbally let the client know that we have ten minutes left, and answer any remaining questions.

Question 2: What will you do to ensure you feel complete?

For instance, I will share my sincere observation around the most important takeaways and make sure to answer them or follow up on any questions that I could not answer.

Great job completing your first rough draft of your outline! It's okay if you feel like there were places you couldn't fill in. What is "missing" will be a great indicator of where you can go to do specific research for your sessions. With this new level of direction for your sessions, you may now shift from trying to learn all of astrology to learning with purpose, one piece at a time.

<u>The next step is to type it up and try it out!</u> In the next chapter, we will work together to create the tools you will need to provide an otherworldly experience. Right now, your outline, when it is truly aligned in your heart, will feel like, "OMG, I can't wait! Whom can I call right now and offer to share this experience with?!?!?!"

Make sure that you are completely connected to your outline before moving forward. This is where you become specific and chose a path. If you are struggling to commit to a singular focus, please remember you are building your vision one step at a time. The outline is not meant to serve you for your entire professional experience working with astrology. It is meant for serving you and your clients now.

SELF-EMPOWERING SACRED TOOLS

As you set yourself up for success, it means becoming intentional on deeper and deeper levels. We made the first outline for your first experience. That was the foundation, but we still have more work to do.

I believe this is why most people resist the Earth pillar. Here you will find that one piece of work often leads to many more pieces of work. Here is the thing: I want you to make it easy on yourself . . . in your sessions! That means the more we prepare and plan now, the easier it will be for you when you go live.

Do you think I printed the astrology charts out and just sat down with clients? Not a chance.

Here is what I did: I created a chart that had all the information built into it. Ponder this fact; in the beginning, I didn't even use astrology symbols! I simply wrote the name of the planet in a circle inside a house. I would download the chart for free online, and then I would transfer the data to my tool that I created to help me read better.

I figured that if I didn't know what the symbols meant, then my client sure didn't know what they meant, and I'd be doing us both a favor! I made tools that supported me in providing the best service I was capable of.

Looking back, I see so clearly that my approach was different. I understood that I was not fluent, but I didn't feel on any level of my *being* that this would prevent me from authentically showing up and sharing what I could. When I knew a technique, I would share it and apply it. I would take one technique, such as the north moon node shows where the soul will grow toward. Then I would sit down with a client, explain the technique, and we would explore the pieces together! We looked at the sign, house, aspects, etc., and by sharing astrology like this, my clients were active participants in their readings.

It was as if, in the beginning, my tools were my training wheels, and without them I wouldn't have been able to share astrology with others. Then one day, I could speak it fluently, but I still break things down like this because it serves the client. I may no longer need a full breakdown, but the client still does.

Training wheels aren't cheating. It's helping you arrive strategically at a future state you desire with more precision. The zodiac signs, houses, and aspects all have keywords associated with them. It can enhance your customer experience by providing this vital information in sessions.

Here are some ways I empowered myself in those early sessions:

I had the archetypes for each zodiac sign on the chart (my tool I created) because it helped me feel secure when I went into the sessions. It served the client as well, because archetypes are easier to relate to versus zodiac signs for most people.

I had the key words of each house written out and would explain the signs, houses, and planets at the beginning of the session. I would often have my client look at all the words in the houses to allow them to connect the dots and see their own interpretation of the data.

Your tools need to support YOU, and they must also provide a powerful experience for your customer. Looking back, I recognize that I created a powerful experience for my clients as I slowed everything down. I may not have been fluent in multiple astrology charts with tons of techniques, but what I did, I did well. I did it from honor and belief in astrology and my desire to be great at interpreting and empowering my clients.

Now it's time to get intimate with your weaknesses and figure out how you can create tools to take the edge off this learning curve. Where are you afraid? Where do you expect you will make a mistake?

Usually, we run from and avoid our fears. We stick it behind us and designate it for a future moment in time to be mastered. I don't recommend this approach. I recommend complete ownership and awareness around what you can and can't do. I still practice this. Why would I ever pretend to be able to do anything beyond what I can do? It is not necessary.

For many out there, you will be able to look at your outline, and you will see the "tool" you need in sections 2 and 3 of your outline. For instance, in reference to the example outline shared in the last chapter, a premade chart with a beautiful image of four elements and the signs with a short description would be a supportive tool for that particular session.

Look back on sections 2 and 3 from your outline and begin to play around with the energy and all the ideas you can come up with for a tool to be used during your sessions. Please don't just settle on the first idea that crosses your mind. I would spend several days, even up to a week, considering and exploring your options. My worksheets from my books are a great example of using a tool to guide your sessions.

Let's work with another example and see what this process looks like . . .

Let's say that the title for the reading is "Your Mood and the Moon." And let's just decide now that the goal is to teach about the connections among the moon, the collective unconscious, and how to track your client's moods with the transiting moon signs. What tools can you think of for this reading? What would you want if you were the client sitting with the astrologer? What happens when you know nothing at all about the moon? How would this shape the experience? What if the client is an expert? How would that shape the experience?

I, for one, would want a one-page moon tracker cheat sheet. I would also like it connected to my birth chart and the houses. That's what I would want as a client with no astrology experience, and it's what I would want as the expert too! Getting into the perspective of the client is important, and that is how you learn to meet their needs. The more you practice this, the easier it gets.

Right now, your job is to get the tool that will remove all "effort energy" from your sessions. We need you to arrive in your session feeling supported, prepared, and like the experience is already created. With the right preparation, all you do is show up and execute.

This is part of the book that falls deeply within your own responsibility to yourself. I can't show up in your room and physically convince you of how awesome tools are. I'm telling you through my words right now that creating a tool to support you and your client is a game changer. It is everything customer service oriented and then some. I can also tell you this: I always have a tool.

Take your time now and pick the tool. Then decide if you want to make it or hire someone else. Many of my simple tools are made in a Word doc and have served me just fine over the years. Commit to setting yourself up for success. Allow your work now to directly elevate you at a future moment in time. Create a sacred partnership with your Future Self.

OPENING PANDORA'S BOX

(WE ALL DO THIS!)

The moment you begin to do this type of work, you will have a domino of many other questions that will start to flow at you. What do I charge? How do I accept payment? Do I need a website? How do I schedule? Where should I meet them? Can I do this online? Do I offer discounts? Do I need social media? Do I record the sessions? The list goes on and on.

When this happens, I know one of two things: one, you have called in the energy big time! You must be making moves if life is making moves back! And two, you entered into a whole other realm that may be completely foreign and new for you.

The energy in most corporate gigs is to look to your superiors and follow them for guidance. We are so ingrained with thinking and feeling that there is someone "above us" that we have a natural tendency to seek out that person. We might even externalize this and think that we need the support of x, y, and z before we can be successful. The truth is that there is no more "above you." You are the boss now.

As the boss of yourself, you will be in charge of everything. Your mind will be flooded with all sorts of thoughts, many of which you have never encountered before. I, for one, am excited for you to take this next step! I believe that stepping into the role of astrologer is a sacred process for those of us who come with our hearts wide open and dedicated to service.

Your outline and your tool need to be fresh on your mind. All the questions that arise will be answered and moved through in perfect timing. Building your skill set isn't something that happens overnight. You will make decisions over and over again. You will change direction and course-correct over and over again.

I provided sessions before I had a website or business cards. I crawled before I walked and walked before I ran. The truth here is that I never viewed either stage as "less than" or "'more than." If you want to enjoy your process, you will have to be happy being where you're at.

Chances are, you will feel a little ambivalent about sharing your services without experience. If you do, thank goodness! It means you are aware and conscious on many deep levels. I felt the same way and did not want to charge until I felt solid in my offering. In the beginning, I provided my services for free to strategically hyperspeed through this phase of the process.

Before we jump into some of my best practices around this, I must share my earlier mistakes and the most-common ones I've seen.

Energetic exchanges: I was once fond of "energetic exchanges." I would be open to swapping with other professionals in our exchange of services. However, on almost every single occasion, this created an energetic mismatch and felt off. In theory, I love this idea, but in practice it tends to make a paradox. I've learned that money does more than we think. Exchanges for the same monetary amount are the highest balanced in this form. For instance, if you charge $50 and exchange with someone who charges $100, you would balance those constraints to make the money equal.

Donation only: We aren't charity. We have a genuine service we provide in the marketplace. I have not personally done this, but I have seen far too many suffer through this mindset. Energetically, this would create a massive tangle. Accepting donations for your work represents an enormous imbalance because it took lifetimes to develop your skill set, and people want to pay you for this. Your ideal client doesn't want the psychic hotline or reading at the fair. They want the professional astrologer. And when you charge for your services, you actually commit to a higher level of service (more of you shows up). If you're not asking for money, it means you are asking for something else. Money is a promise between two people. As long as you deliver on your end, the money will flow to you and will empower both you and your clients.

We need to recognize that we all walk through this dark night of the soul "business edition": from fear of charging into charging for our services.

Here is my current best practice around this phase of growth: First, decide on what your price will be, and lock that price in energetically. Maybe you will start with $55 an hour, $110 an hour, $250 an hour, etc. Rather than just trying to "feel" your way to the right number, do some market research to see how much people are charging. We want the mind and heart working together, and though there is much research into price numbers that sell better, I have found that when I feel aligned with my pricing on the basis of being competitive with the other prices for similar services in the marketplace, my customers also feel comfortable and confident. Write this price down and let it be known. If someone asks you, "I have a friend who would love this. What do you charge?," you will be ready and available to answer that question unflustered.

Decide and hold your price steady until you feel you must raise it. It could be one year from now or two years. You will know when the time is right, but you must hold it steady. If you have no clue what to charge, do market research and see what others are charging.

Once you have locked in your price, all you need to do is the following assignment:

Assignment: Find five to ten people to share your session with in exchange for a written testimonial that can be shared on your website.

This is your assignment, and you absolutely can do this. Your focus is to find five to ten people and say, "Hey, I'm starting to do moon readings. I am looking for volunteers to do a session with me in exchange for a written testimonial. Would this be something you might be interested in?"

Do you know how in Mario Kart, if you hit the go button at the right time, you get that superspeed? I feel like this little container that allows you to develop, gather testimonials, and serve simultaneously is that superspeed boost you need. Once you've completed this phase, you will charge for your services, and since you will have already moved through your outline multiple times, you will feel 150 percent ready when you are providing your services professionally.

YOUR POINT OF RESISTANCE AND HOW TO OVERCOME IT

If you have studied spiritual disciplines, you will know that living on Earth is a spiritual training ground. It is my personal belief that many spirits come here by choice, while other souls are currently being birthed here into the physical for the very first time. In my early meditations, I was shown that planet Earth was the cosmic birthing ground of all the cosmos. It is the innermost world of creation, and though many "entities" may try to alter its path, it is cosmically guarded through powerful universal laws.

It's time for us to finish working with the energies of the Earth pillar and enter into the Air pillar. Technically, you are not IN the Air pillar until you have physically practiced your outline with clients here on physical Earth. Visualize all you want, but you do not enter into the next phases of the creation process until you bring the Earth pillar fully manifest.

As you progress through the creative pillars, you will hit your resistance point. A resistance point in the creative process often will put you in an *energetic loop*. Typically, this is felt inside your body like you are a hamster on a wheel. Like you are "doing all the right things" but never progressing. This space can feel extremely frustrating, and it is often very misleading. It is like being in the maze without an "observer self" that can properly guide you.

So when you do hit a resistance point, please write it down and figure out where you resist. You must first start by identifying which element you are in resistance to. For some, the resistance point will feel like a "block." Kind of like a "I don't want to do that." Or it sounds more like, "We need to study a little bit longer." Or you may be hearing things like, "No need to rush into anything. I'll wait until the right time."

That is what I call a "traditional block." It's like coming up to a dead end and then retracing the same movement that led up to it over and over again rather than looking for creative ways to move around, through, above, or below the block in the path.

There is also an opposite presentation of the resistance point that many people miss. It appears in a counterintuitive way and feels like you are trying to "speed things up" or move through a phase of the process *quickly*. Here you don't passively avoid the block, but you instinctually attempt to bulldoze it with your willpower.

It will feel like you are "rushing the process" or "using your willpower and force." This type of energy loop accounts for creations not sticking or not building momentum. It's almost like a collapsing occurs internally because you are *hopping* or *phasing* through a step of the process.

Here is a bit of what I know about what it feels like to be resistant to a phase:

FIRE RESISTANCE

If you resist Fire, you will often put down your ideas and not even give them a chance. If I were to say to you, "Come up with five ways to share the zodiac," you would roll your eyes and think what a dull exercise. It is like the mind thinks there is only "one right answer" and you have a short circuit somewhere that will say, "Don't even bother trying." The resistance here prevents you from generating the initial momentum that can propel you forward through the creative process. Applied outside astrology to love, it is when you refuse to even date but grow resentful that you haven't met your mate yet.

EARTH RESISTANCE

If you resist Earth, you might hear yourself say things like, "That is overkill, and no one needs to put that much *effort* in." You will go to sit down to do the work, and it won't come easily, and instead of going inward, you push outward, saying, "This is a waste of time! They are just trying to fill pages in a book, and this exercise is useless; give me the good stuff!" The ego here is resentful and doesn't want to put in *effort* without a guarantee that it will work out. Outside astrology, this is when you have great ideas but assume no one will listen, so you never take the time to write a proposal and approach your boss with your idea.

AIR RESISTANCE

If you resist Air, there will be resistance around your identity and often fear or anxiety around how others perceive you.

When it comes to taking a step back and seeking to elevate as Air, you will have a fear of appearing controlling, manipulative, needy, egotistical, and then some. Because of this, shifting gears feels like a big deal, even though it is a necessary part of evolution. You might fear that you will let others down or that they will judge you for the decisions you are making. Here is a great example of someone resisting Air: Let's say a store owner notices that employees are taking lunch breaks that are too long, and it's hurting the business. The store owner realizes the solution might be having the employee clock in and out for lunch to solve the labor problem. The store owner's resistance would most likely manifest as hesitation, and the thought would be something like, "It will cost too much to implement, and there must be an easier way." The truth is, there is a refusal to elevate. Clocking in and out and setting new expectations with the employees would most likely cause some sort of energetic conflict. On some level, we all know these things, and thus the resistance to Air.

WATER RESISTANCE

The resistance to Water is resistance to stillness, silence, healing. There is a fear of turning yourself "off." You struggle to separate from your creation or goal and thus inadvertently stunt the growth through the creative process. When you sit down to relax, you will feel waves of guilt that you "should be doing something else" or that "everything will fall apart" or that you "should wait to rest once everything is up and running perfectly." It is connected to taking on too much responsibility and needing to learn how to provide and care for yourself as you would care for others. This is seen outside astrology when people refuse to put their phones down and literally believe that "things will fall apart without them" and that they must always remain "available."

Knowledge is power, and the more you know, understand, and accept how you work through the pillars of creation, the better you will be at working with that energy. It has not been my experience that we outgrow our resistance points, but rather that we learn to manage and adapt. We seek to bring in people who help us with our weaknesses, and we, in turn, get to share our strengths.

What do you think your strengths are? What are your weaknesses?

I want you to spend a moment reflecting on what we've covered so far in this book.

IN THE FIRE SECTION:

Chapter 1: We worked on accepting the job. We shifted from the energy of "the astrology student" into the "new astrologer."

Chapter 2: We activated the seedling blueprint and locked it at the moment in time where this journey began. You learned that it is a living, breathing, flexible plan, and this is why it is impossible to "fully download" how it will unfold.

Chapter 3: We worked to distinguish the role of astrology versus the astrologer. In accepting that we are interpreters, we allow astrology to do the heavy lifting, and we support others to work with it in their lives.

Chapter 4: We selected your starting point that would be the basis for the rest of the work in the book. This is a piece of astrology that you feel strongly magnetized to, and will be the central focus of your initial readings. We accept that astrology is not a separate path but will merge with the gifts, talents, and skills you already have.

IN THE EARTH SECTION:

Chapter 5: We homed in deeper on your starting point and built your first experience, using my outline template. The outline aims to create consistency and provide the structure you need to support, train, and develop yourself as you grow.

Chapter 6: We picked out a sacred tool that you could develop to support you and your client in your sessions. The tool allows you to feel confident and simultaneously deepens the experience your client will receive. It is your "training wheels."

Chapter 7: We selected a price and created a safe container to promote your growth as you pass through the "teenage years" into accepting payments for your service. The assignment is to find five to ten people to share your service with in exchange for a testimonial.

This catches us up to chapter 8, where we are right now. We looked at the resistance points that we all hit within our pillars. Right now, I would expect that you have completed the following:

1: You have an outline that lights up your soul and excites you! It's an "OMG! This will be so fun to share, and I simply cannot wait to sit down with a client and share this with them."

2: You have a tool (created by you or outsourced) that you just know on deep levels will support you and your clients as you share with them during your sessions. It makes you feel safe, supported, guided, and calm.

3: You have asked five to ten people if they would be willing to receive a free session from you in exchange for a testimonial.

Most likely, you have hesitated a bit on the third piece mentioned above. Maybe you have asked one person and are waiting to hear back. Maybe you haven't asked yet. This is a very common "energetic hiccup" (and often why one would seek out an astrologer coach like me to help them move through it).

This activity is the point of commitment for the ego. It is the point of saying, "Hey, we're doing this thing! Regardless of what other people say or do!" Any doubts you have about choosing this path will begin to surface at this point. It is natural and normal to feel this way and to have doubts about how it will all work out.

Here is my recommendation and what I did to make it through this: I always came back to the truth and asked, "Do I want to be an astrologer?" When I ask this, it shifts me from having to know the plan for success, which I couldn't know, back to what I actually can know: "Do I want this?"

If this is 150 percent for you and you want this, I recommend you jump into the deep end of the pool. Don't just dip your toe in to see how it feels. Jump. Don't ask one person at a time. Ask five people at a time. The magic in conversions and creating confidence isn't taking baby steps and trying to balance your micromovements. You need macrolevel movements, and within that approach, you grow more efficiently.

In my opinion, asking one person at a time is a bad approach in this circumstance. Think about it mathematically. Let's say you have a list of five people. Spirit already knows that three are saying no and two are saying yes. Which path appeals more to you? The one where you ask one person a week and rack up three nos before a single yes? Or would you prefer doing it all in one day and getting three nos and two yesses?

In business, you have to look at sample sizes and margins. Asking one person at a time may seem more manageable for the task load, but for the "emotional load," it isn't. This new way of looking at things is the Air phase of the creative process, and we are going there next! But first, make sure you have reached out to a minimum of five people to offer them the incredible opportunity for you to share astrology with them. Don't skip this. Please trust yourself and empower yourself. If everyone says no, you will survive that, and that "no" can actually fuel you. When something doesn't work for me, more creative energy flows to me and through me, and I am presented with the most-amazing ideas. Allow the process to work and give it a chance.

If I was with you right now, I would sit down with you and look at your outline and tools. I would help you find cohesion and connect the dots. I would allow you a safe place to practice your work and provide you with written and live feedback. Some may need this extra support, and others will not. If you do need extra support, please email me at emily@absolutelyastrology.com. Though I cannot provide my feedback free of charge, I have a training program that can support you and provide you with one-on-one access to me.

PILLAR 3 OF THE CREATIVE PROCESS:

ELEVATE IT (AIR)

In this phase, you are in a state of elevation. You are ready to take a step back and analyze the work you have done. You are eager to detach from the original vision so that you can take it to a new height. In fact, you change the original vision and start to explore all the possibilities.

This energy courses through you and makes you feel like every challenge has a solution. You continually adapt and make the necessary changes to your original vision. If you resist the energy of Pillar 4 (Elevate It), the more at risk you are for overchanging. You risk losing connection to the original vision, and your momentum will slip.

ELEVATING YOUR SERVICE EACH AND EVERY TIME

I want to ask you a question. So here we go: "From an energetic perspective, what is the most important part of your interaction with a client?"

Pause. Breathe. Then respond.

I need you to sit with this for a second and think about it (that's why I haven't answered it already!). What could it be? Is it the end of the interaction when you sum everything up? Is it when you deliver the astrology interpretation? Is it in the future, when they listen to the recording ten years later and everything came true?

I don't think I would ever be able to answer when the most important part of the interaction happens for the client, but I do know for certain what the most important piece of the interaction is for me. It happens in the first five minutes, when I take the time to get to know my clients, and I listen and seek to figure out the exact reason they have come to see me.

Every interaction starts with a warm greeting and sacred questions. This is how you breathe Air into your service and elevate it.

Remember in section 1 of your outline, when you came up with some questions you could ask your client? Those questions are sacred, and this is the most important stage of every interaction. This is how you will determine why your paths have crossed, the important message you are meant to deliver, and how to infuse the whole interaction with love.

If you have created a "Moon and Your Moods" experience and someone signs up, you have one very important piece of knowledge: the client is interested in the moon and their moods. This is a good first step in understanding your client, but it could never be enough to truly inspire another soul.

I want to show you the impact that can happen when you take time at the beginning of the interaction to ask open-ended sacred questions. We will apply this to our hypothetical reading titled "The Moon and Your Moods." Here are just a few possible sacred questions:

"I'm curious; are there any moods in particular that you have a hard time processing? Is there a mood you don't often express?"

"Before we get started, I was wondering, do you currently track your moods? How do you do this? Has this been helpful?"

Most people don't ask enough questions, and when they do, they accidentally ask questions that close energy rather than open it. If someone asks, "Have you gone to a moon class before?," you energetically end up in a different place than if you asked, "I'm curious; are there any moods in particular that you have a hard time processing? Is there a mood you don't often express?" A good question gets someone excited about their response.

Through the questions you ask, you will discover why your client truly came to you. If you don't ask sacred questions, you will never truly know. For me, I love knowing why people want to work with astrology. Within five minutes, I am capable of discerning the true intention of why someone has shown up in my world. I have many open-ended sacred questions I can ask, and I use a combination of my intuition and my mind to decide which ones.

Let me show you how this information will energetically infuse your sessions with individualized purpose and meaning:

MEET CLIENT CLAUDIA

Through your sacred open-ended questions, you discover that Claudia's mom was an astrologer who read her chart for her as a kid. Claudia has always been fascinated by it, but slightly scared because it brings up issues from her childhood. She is trying to move past this and wants to start working with the moon. A friend recommended this to her, and that friend also recommended you specifically. She shares that she has trouble expressing anger, and this is something she is working on.

MEET CLIENT SAMANTHA

Through your qualifying open-ended questions, you discover that Samantha is a midwife, and she is interested in the moon because of the correlation she has seen in her own work. She has noted differences in delivery based on the moon, and it is very interesting to her. She is ambivalent about sharing this information with others and wants to work with the moon only on a deeply personal basis. She has just recalled a childhood memory in therapy, and she is trying to heal herself. She read online that the moon has a feminine quality, and a friend recommended you.

Please think about how you would change your approach for each of these clients; what would you change or do differently? Think about what would happen if you shared the outline the exact same way without adapting to their needs; would this help or hinder the experience? Please also take a moment to consider how your energy is impacted by knowing their true story and the real reason they came to work with you. Are you more excited? More confident? Do you feel you can truly serve?

For me, it's the story of the client that lights up my soul.

Here is what I mean: With Claudia, I would have heard that anger was hard for her to process. I would have thus encouraged awareness and connecting with it through the collective first. I most likely would look at the Fire signs with more depth and have her watch her moods when the moon is in Aries, Leo, or Sagittarius. I'd help her using the worksheet and mark the dates for her. With that little bit of information she gave me, I believe I could transform a reading from "That was cool" to "She changed my life."

For Samantha, I might trace the initial childhood memory down by date and explore the moon sign and phase at that time. I might help her look for that pattern and suggest she do healing work for herself on those specific days. Perhaps she plans her trip to the nail salon or her therapy sessions to align with that energy to move it through her body and out. I would really try to figure out how to customize the reading to meet her needs.

Do you see how astrology is still doing the astrology? But can you see how the information you gather at the beginning of the reading will and can alter the experience from being good to being life altering?

> In every session, you have the opportunity to learn just as much as your client does. "

In your outline, you wrote a few questions in section 1. We need to elevate now and return to those questions. Our goal is to refine them, expand them, and ensure that they are sacred to the experience. Please pull out your outline and see what you wrote. Then I want you to activate some Air!

STEP 1: Take some time to come up with five open-ended sacred questions that are relevant to your material within the outline. Update your outline with the new, intentional sacred questions.

STEP 2: Test out your questions by sharing a few of these questions in your sessions where you are gathering your testimonials. Seek to discover which questions bring you the most-relevant information. Be aware not to accidentally bombard your client with too many questions, or you will frustrate them.

There is a "hit or miss" quality when it comes to infusing Air into the creative process. That is to say, you won't know which questions are truly sacred until you see them at work. I have taught many workshops in my life, and it is very curious how some questions "land" and others do not. The trick here is not to personalize it and beat yourself up. It's to tell yourself, "It's a question. I can change a question."

One of the most powerful questions I have asked that virtually everyone loves is "If you could go backward in time and meet your ancestors or forward in time and meet your descendants, which would you chose and why?" I got this question from a blog and adapted it over time, slowly testing different variations. This one was my winner, and it is my go-to for group workshop icebreakers.

You wouldn't believe the answers and stories I have heard! And here is something interesting: if you drop the "and why?," you'll change it to an energetic closed-ended question. Two words can take a question from so-so to life altering. You really can be two words away from having a perfect question that opens the heart.

You can go further with this, and I always do! If you are inspired, try playing around with asking more-profound and open-ended questions to those whom you love and admire. When you meet with your boss, seek to ask a sacred open-ended question like "I don't think you've ever told me, but what was it that drew you to this line of work?" Watch how the right question at the right time can open a heart.

I do have one warning—never ever ask a question you don't truly desire to hear the answer to. To open a door and not meet someone there in service is dangerous energy. Ask sacred questions at sacred times to those whom you hold sacred in your world.

MULTIDIMENSIONAL ENGAGEMENT: WHERE YOU AND YOUR CLIENT WIN

Our beliefs are shaping every experience, for better or for worse. And we must be responsible for our own beliefs about ourselves. You have strong beliefs deep inside you that will either serve you or not when it comes to your interactions. By simply becoming aware of them, you activate your Air element, and you elevate your service BEFORE it begins.

In the last chapter, I really wanted to open you up to the importance of the first five minutes you spend with your client. I am hoping that you deeply understand that the qualifying sacred questions you ask during that time will be able to anchor and ground the rest of the reading. I recommend updating your outline as we continue your training through the book.

The truth is that success is already in motion before it happens. You must have the right energy inside you before you see it manifest outside you. I want to share some of my beliefs that I hold around the role I play as an astrologer, so that you might consider them for yourself. There is no pressure, just my sincere offering to help you establish your role. All of my beliefs come from my life experience, and not a single one was learned in a day, but they are sacred to me, and I hope that they may be sacred for you.

Here they are:

Astrology is sacred to me.
It is my honor to share.
I'm 150 percent ready and prepared.
I am willing to adapt.
I am open and receptive.
I can trust my clients to tell me the truth; I will believe what they say.
I can trust that my client has come to me at the right time in their life.

I can trust that my client wants me to share astrology with them.

I can trust that my client knows whether or not to hire me.

I can trust that my client was brought to me by God.

When you come to a client interaction with a proper outline, when your beliefs are solid and your energy is good, plus you are asking your qualifying sacred questions, I believe that dynamic engagement becomes effortless. This means the following:

The conversation will flow, and there will be an ease in the interaction.

You will feel centered and balanced, and your client will come into center/balance through the experience.

Body language will be open and engaging with multiple displays of various emotions.

There will be questions and spontaneity, and it will not feel rehearsed.

Remember, if you are not engaged, your client won't be engaged. If you don't feel that astrology is sacred, your client won't feel that astrology is sacred. If you don't trust your client, your client won't trust you. Your client will reflect your beliefs (for the most part) and treat your work the same way that you do.

> Your energy = Your beliefs = The energy that charges the container

I have found over the years that my beliefs can stabilize a container. That is to say, someone comes to me in one feeling space and leaves in another because I energetically hold the space. This happens because I can consistently bring the same energy into my readings, and I prepare the exact same way for every single client.

Here are my beliefs in action, fully crystallized as truth through my consistent behaviors:

It is true that I will never drink and be hung over for a session, and I will never put myself in a situation that will compromise my mood leading up to a reading (**Belief:** astrology is sacred to me).

It is true that I am never late, and I begin working charts thirty minutes before I meet with a client (**Belief:** I am 150 percent prepared).

It is true that I have a clean workspace and fresh water for me to drink during the session, and I use incense and candles to set the mood and prepare myself to show up fully through my work (**Belief:** I am open and receptive).

It is true that my space looks clean and professional; I look the part and I don't show up in my underwear (**Belief:** it is my honor to share).

My beliefs inform my actions, and my actions inform my beliefs. When someone has the power to make you question yourself, there is something shaky within your belief system. The stronger the belief, the less likely someone can get under your skin. There isn't a single soul in this world that could make me doubt that astrology is sacred. With my beliefs so strongly in place, most people do not intentionally waste their time trying to change my mind, because on a deep unconscious level, they already know it is not possible.

Here is one thing that I have learned after ten years in customer service: When your energy field is strong, your clients will match your field. This means that they will take on your strength and feel it as their own. They will feel stable and comfortable if you feel stable and comfortable. When you respect your time, they respect your time. Your client is responding to you on many levels; your job is to ensure you have set yourself up for success physically, mentally, and emotionally.

I want you to think about what you must do to set yourself up for success; what is it for you? I have trained lots of people over the years, and it is different for every person. Sometimes it meant committing to working out, because that was their key. For others, it was a thirty-minute meditation in the morning. There is no recipe here, but rather a commitment to taking care of yourself and ensuring that you come as your best self into your interactions.

What are your current beliefs? And are they serving you? How does it feel about writing them out and interacting with them? Questioning them? Evolving them?

What can you do to make sure you come feeling prepared, balanced, and whole? What will be an expectation you can set for yourself that will ultimately lead to your inevitable success?

One belief I have worked on often with people is "I need to know everything." As you might imagine, this belief is not in service to the client or to the person holding the belief. It is literally an impossibility to know everything, and thus it is a false belief. These happen all the time, and luckily they are the easiest to break because they have no truth within them.

I faced that belief long ago in my earlier years working for Lush. If you've ever seen the amount of product and the list of ingredients within a Lush store, you can imagine how that belief was formed in my mind! I thought I had to know everything, and yet, a hop, skip, and a jump away was this: "I am willing to find that information out for you." And with that new belief, the creative force of Air was breathed into me, and I was able to let go, release the unnecessary pressure, and simply do my best.

Right now, what five beliefs can you bring with you on your journey? Add these to your outline at the top as a reminder to yourself. The outline is yours, and please do not share it with clients. It is safe to write them there at the top, and we will be adding more things now to the bottom.

SETTING YOURSELF UP FOR SUCCESS

The process your client moves through, from the first point of contact until they are in their reading with you, is your responsibility; it's your process.

I want you to imagine that you signed up and purchased a reading from someone, but you didn't receive a confirmation email. Let's say you wait a day, and still nothing. You reach out by email, and two days later the person responds and says, "Yes, I have you confirmed."

Let's also pretend that they give you no details. Here you are wondering, "Do I need to do anything to prepare? How will I log in?" Then a few hours before the reading, you get a short email that says, "Please use this link to log on for your session."

What sort of impression was communicated through this process? Whatever it is, it's not good.

Good customer service happens before, during, and after the purchase. Seeing this and owning it, that's the Air pillar. We are now stepping back from your interaction so that we can see the whole process: beginning, middle, and end. With all the wonderful energy you have poured into your outline and into developing your reading, it is full of great customer service. Your open-ended sacred questions combined with bringing the right energy through your beliefs are straight gold.

Right now, we need to take it one step further and extend the intention into the before, during, and after of how you will share astrology with the world. We need to fuel the whole process with the intention to serve and help your clients. When you do this well, your job as an astrologer becomes much easier, the experience gets elevated (even more), and you begin to attract clients versus tracking them down.

Right now, I want you to practice flipping your energy into the customer's mindset. When we do this, we can solve all the possible problems that might exist for your client before they occur. Fun, isn't it? By thinking as the customer would, you can then fill in the blanks and ensure that your process meets their needs.

To help illustrate this process, I'm going to share the questions I believe are swirling about in the mind of someone considering working with me:

Who is this person, and what does she do?
How does a session work, and what is the financial fee?
What information do I need to have for an astrology reading, and how do I get that information?
Is it safe to share birth data, and can I trust this person?
What will I get out of this experience? What can they actually teach me?
Is this for real, or is it just for fun?
Is this the right time for me to do this?

Those questions are very conscious. Let's go deeper and look at what I believe are the unconscious thoughts of the potential client:

Is it going to be easy for me to book this reading?
Is it going to be easy for me emotionally? Technically? Physically?
Is it going to be easy for me to understand? Do I have to know astrology to benefit from this?
Can I trust this person with this information?

How will my situation be treated?

Is this something that I can afford? How will I be able to pay? All at once? A deposit?

How will I get to and where do I go for this reading? Is it safe?

What do other people think about working with astrology?

Right now, I want you to look through these customer questions and ask yourself, "Are these reasonable questions?" I mean, do you think that these are probable and natural questions that will most likely be asked of you? I think yes; these questions are likely to surface.

There could be a hundred more questions, but that isn't the point. The point is that you narrow in on the most-likely questions that you will run into. This way, you will be prepared, and you will have the answer ready when someone asks you. A great best practice is to create a template for yourself that answers these questions, which you cut and paste from when you are communicating with clients by email. It creates consistency in your customer service, and it is less time consuming than searching for links or typing the same thing over and over again.

Right now, I want you to grab a piece of paper and something to write with and try to get into the mindset of your potential customer. Please know, we may be serving wildly different audiences, and my questions may not fit. For instance, if the service is "Mom and Baby Readings," you will have different questions than I do. The first one that pops into my mind is "When is the right time to get the reading? Before the baby is born or after?"

Play with this and have fun with this. Go inward and try to feel your way through and understand that perspective. This exercise is some of my favorite energy work: transcending your own ego and learning to see from another perspective. It is Air in service to your customer.

Once you get all the questions, type them into the bottom of your outline. Then, over the remainder of the book, ensure that you take the time to answer these questions (and if you can't, you take the initiative to figure out the answer). This is awesome, and it is called path paving. You are working with the energy in a new way now, preparing in advance, and making the process of receiving fluid and natural.

CONVERSIONS = CONNECTION

Of all the business metrics, conversions teach us the most about the level of customer service in a business. Conversions measure the amount of people who commit to either a purchase or a sign up. If ten people visit your website, and four people sign up, you have a 40 percent conversion rate. If you ask twenty people to join your email list, and ten people sign up, you have a 50 percent conversion rate. If five out of ten of your clients return to you year after year, you have a 50 percent conversion for repeat clientele. Zero conversion means there is no connection/flow/synergy between your material and your audience. The higher the conversion, the more connection/flow/synergy.

When I teach workshops, I look at the number of people who attend the workshop and see who takes the initiative to work with me one on one in an astrology reading. This allows me to gauge how compelling my material is from within my workshop. Conversions always reflect the activity that precedes it (remember that!).

It's a bit tricky because when something isn't converting, you might not know why. This is where you need to call in the Air element, which likes to solve mysteries and problems. If you've ever been close friends with people who have their sun in Gemini, Libra, or Aquarius, you might have noticed that they perk up when a challenge arises. They are the first to try to figure things out, and they always see multiple solutions.

Long ago, when I was first starting out, my mind would ask these silly, unproductive questions when conversions were low. I'm guessing you can relate or might relate to this at some point on your journey:

Why isn't anyone excited about what I'm doing?
Why are my sales low? Why isn't anyone buying?
What am I doing wrong? Why can't I figure this
out?

You may have asked yourself these insane questions as well (or something like it). These questions are a recipe for disaster and not a good choice. They will pin the responsibility back into your energetic field, and this is no good because it is simply NOT true. The truth here is that when you ask questions like these, you will get answers that feed into that same level of thinking.

You will be running around like a chicken with your head cut off because you aren't actually focusing your very strong mind in the right way. Try these new questions out and see how they feel:

What am I doing to engage with my audience and
have fun with them?

What am I doing to train and nourish my soul?
How can I nourish others?

What are other ways I might repackage this and
try again?

With better questions, you will get better answers. And as you move along your path, you will be able to identify how you can support yourself.

Earlier in the book, I asked you to start by sharing astrology with five to ten individuals in exchange for a testimonial. This was a strategic move to build your skill set, gather confidence, and prepare for when you are charging for your services. I'm hoping you have tested out your outline and begun the process of Air, where you begin to tweak, change, and update your outline.

If, for some reason, you are struggling with this and no one is saying, "Yes!," please don't panic. The last thing I would ever want is for you to think that a few nos is a sign that you are on the wrong path. Take it from someone with a sales and customer service background; you will get plenty of nos on the journey, but it doesn't necessarily mean that you have a bad product or service. Sometimes, it's simply that you are marketing to the wrong audience. Meaning, you're trying to sell meat to a vegan.

Whenever I have a situation when I'm not converting, I like to circle back around to my energy, my intention, my material, and, finally, my audience. It's how I check for energy leaks and troubleshoot to help me get to those better questions mentioned earlier that will be the key to figuring out my next steps.

Here are a few helpful questions you can ask yourself if you are not converting:

Question #1: Am I beyond excited to share my reading with the world? Does it light up my soul and make me a bit anxious and nervous, but mostly profoundly excited?

Question #2: Does the title sell the course? Does the title of the outline sum it up perfectly and allow someone to feel what it will be like in a reading with me?

Question #3: Do I feel firm in my beliefs and expectations of myself? Have I written them down and committed them to paper?

Question #4: Who is my current audience? Do I genuinely and with all the passion from my heart desire to serve this particular audience?

Those questions I posed are all a "heck yes" from me. I am beyond excited to share astrology with new astrologers; I literally love the title of this book! It feels like an employee handbook, and I feel firm in my beliefs, and I cannot think of a more worthy, inspiring, and perfect group of souls to share my knowledge with than the new astrologers of the Aquarian Age.

Some things in this world you can't fake. You need to have those ducks in a row, develop the service, as I have pointed out, and get in front of the right audience. Only you have these answers for yourself. I can show up and give you the steps, but deep within you is the truth. If you aren't 100 percent "yes" about the above, it means you need to work the process again.

You might need to update the outline or throw it out. I've thrown out tons of work that hasn't been successful for me over the years. I do it because I know it did serve me. It helped me gain clarity, and if I didn't try, I would have never known.

Once you are a total "Yes!" to all those questions, you just have to move into spaces that reach your ideal audience. Think about the "Mom and Child" reading. You would know your audience is new moms, and your work is to figure out how to connect or share your services with that group. You could try placing a flyer at a local "Mommy and Me" class, or maybe go to an independent boutique baby store that sells infant clothes, and chat up the owner and offer to do a free class.

Sometimes people think it is magic what I've done. Sometimes, they think that I got lucky. For me personally, when someone thinks I got lucky or makes comments like that to me, it cuts me to my core. The reason it cuts me is that it's a lie, and that particular lie hurts them more than it hurts me. And it cuts because I know there is not a single word I can say to help them. They see luck, and it's not for me to change that mindset (that's God's work). Hard work over time looks like luck. Hard work, in the beginning, is how I look effortless in my delivery now. There is no here without there.

We are about to leave behind the Air pillar and move into Water. The goal with Air was to elevate your readings and take you to new heights. Let's do a quick review.

> The options are endless once you know the audience and you have all your ducks in a row.

Chapter 9: We learned about the power of asking sacred questions to your clients within the first five minutes of your readings. I had you add five open-ended sacred questions to your outline, and asked that you practice sharing them so that you might narrow them down to the ones that are most effective.

Chapter 10: We explored the power of beliefs and setting yourself up for success to ensure you enter your interactions from a place of power. You were to write out five beliefs at the top of your outline to remind yourself, and I pointed out that it is your real-life behaviors that bring them to life.

Chapter 11: We had some fun getting into the mindset of the customer and learning how to perfect your process. You journaled out the questions relevant to your audience and spent some time answering them, and creating a Q&A template at the bottom of your outline.

Chapter 12: We discussed the power of conversions and how to know what to do if you are not selling your product/service as you had hoped. I walked you through my process of finding energetic leaks and emphasized the importance of loving and connecting with your audience.

Air energy within the creative process will always be about refining, revisiting, and shifting. Alas, we cannot get stuck here tinkering with things forever. We must move forward into the healing depths of Water. We must give ourselves permission to surrender and let go. We must allow God to move us, guide us, and set our creations free.

Let's go there now. Let us intentionally heal and restore ourselves and break free from the need to produce.

PILLAR 4 OF THE CREATIVE PROCESS:

GIVE IT MEANING (WATER)

In this phase, you are seeking to create meaning for your work by surrendering control of the outcome. You realize the importance of enjoying your whole life, and you begin to reassess your emotional state, and you seek inner connection with your Source. You go inward. You question. You seek the bigger meaning.

This energy courses through you and makes you feel like Spirit has called you home to reconnect with your soul. If you resist the energy of Pillar 1 (the Vision), you will find that you are in the cocoon phase too long. You hesitate and pause. You overthink and feel as if things aren't "right enough" to proceed.

HAVING HEALTHFUL BOUNDARIES

(WITH CLIENTS AND YOURSELF!)

We have moved through Fire and worked our intentions. We have grounded in Earth, and we have elevated in Air. We are now entering the Water pillar of the creative process—a place where we focus on ourselves, healing, restoration, and love. You are amazing for doing this work and stepping up to the plate. Working with astrology and sharing it with the world is a gift. For the remainder of the book, I'm sharing the ways I work with Water and how I heal.

We will start here at the epicenter: relationships and boundaries—the ultimate form of self-protection and self-respect.

Let's go inward and get started:

THE SUN
(THE CENTER OF YOU):

If the universe was inside you (which it is!), you are the sun. If you ever wondered *why* you could explode relationships, it's because nothing can exist in the space with your sun. This is your center. Your *beingness*. It is your responsibility to know you're the sun and not to guide people into your sun. Your consciousness is witnessing this life and influencing it twenty-four hours a day, seven days a week, 365 days a year.

The crystallization of the sun is your name, personality construct, and physical voice.

Your sun is polarizing and is the central force of your inner world. Some things, people, and life simply cannot exist within proximity to your sun. There are people on Earth who literally would never even be able to meet *you*. Your sun can inspire people, grow people, love people, connect to people.

There will occasionally be some things, people, and life that will climb toward your sun and accidentally *get inside it*. This happens more and more as you shine your light out, take ownership of, and truly express your authentic self.

When this occurs, people often blow themselves up or randomly explode, and a relationship will end. This can be painful if you don't understand that it serves you both at the same time. This is because if anyone sees their sun outside themselves (and in someone else), they are in a very important stage of self-awakening. The explosion sends them home to their own universe, where they can focus on their own sun. There is rhyme and reason, a time and a season.

It is 100 percent your responsibility and your right to protect, own, love, and nourish your sun. It is not selfish or wrong to have awareness around the importance of your sun, your essence in your world. You must work for your sun and consciously choose whom you let orbit you and maintain the health of your solar system (life).

If you feel completely drained energetically of your life force, you need to explore this aspect of *being*. Look at the sun in your chart and the aspects to it. Help empower yourself through this energy. For a more in-depth analysis, I recommend my Astrologer Training Program, available at www.absolutelyastrology.com.

> When your sun is healthy, your body will feel healthy: physically, emotionally, mentally.

MERCURY (THE FIRST ORBIT OUT FROM YOUR SUN)

Since no one can exist in your sun with you, the next closest thing is your Mercury orbit. Imagine that the closer the planet (a.k.a. person) that orbits your sun, the more integrated they are into your life. I find that the people in my Mercury orbit are my husband, children, and pets. These are the only people who see me and communicate with me on a daily basis. If something changes in one of our lives, it changes in all of our lives.

I always say, "My husband is my Mercury, and I am his." We are in the closest orbit to each other, but we don't enter into each other's consciousness, since we are both owning our suns simultaneously. This holds us in a multidimensional orbit. I orbit him, and he orbits me at the same time, in the same way.

This is also the place where we communicate and give voice to our thoughts. Speaking your truth and owning your voice are required within the Mercury orbit. If you struggle in close personal relationships or through marketing or advertising, seek to understand Mercury in your chart and all aspects made to it. For a more in-depth analysis, I recommend my Astrologer Training Program, available at www.absolutelyastrology.com.

VENUS
(THE SECOND ORBIT OUT
FROM THE SUN)

The Venus orbit, for me, belongs to those whom I am close to, where time can pass and I always feel like I just saw them. I mean, I have some friends where it could be two years, and then I see them, and it feels like we were just together. The Venus orbit in your world is an earned place, and I believe it is earned through multiple lifetimes. I don't grant people access to this place within my world—they kind of just settle into it as if they've always been there.

This is where we feel supported, loved, seen, and heard.

It is a place of comfort within ourselves, but we don't do it on the daily. We might at times mistakenly try to place people in our Venus orbit, but I don't think we can consciously set up these relationships. For me, they are 150 percent karmic and a dynamic that transcends a single life. You can't mess these relationships up, because they are built in the etheric. They grow back together, and even when you fight, you still love one another and hold space for coming back together (in this life or the next!).

How you give and receive love is connected to your Venus energy in your chart. I find that we like to be loved in certain ways, and we attract people as such. The goal is that you can love them back in the ways they like to be loved as well. For a more in-depth analysis, I recommend my Astrologer Training Program, available at www. absolutelyastrology.com.

EARTH (YOUR PHYSICAL BODY)

Your body is your piece of Earth. The moon orbits the earth and represents the aspects of self that are still integrating within you. There can be things happening inside your universe that you are not consciously aware of. This is largely to protect your ego so that it can grow and crystallize. Over time, you will integrate more aspects of self.

Your body is always communicating with you and needs your support on this journey. How you treat and honor your body is reflective of how you are treating yourself internally. This can be hard to see at times, but the truth is that the body is a tool. It is the *Spirit* inside the body that is being grown here on Earth, and the body often expresses the happenings of the sun, moon, Mercury, and Venus energy within.

ALL OTHER OUTER ORBITS

Your universe is your universe. What and how you hold each of the orbits is completely up to you. I just know that they exist and can help you in navigating relationships personally and professionally.

Beyond the earth, we have many more orbits. I like to work backward at this point and move from Pluto back to Mars. That is how the energy feels to me INSIDE, and thus I'm sharing it that way with you right now.

PLUTO

People who know me, but whom I do not know. If you have a hard time feeling like you have the ability to transform, work with the aspects of this planet for help.

URANUS

People who skip into and out of my life for short stints but are very remarkable, and there are no ill feelings when we "move on." If you fail to embrace the spontaneous in your life and feel like synchronicities aren't showing up, you will need to do more digging here.

NEPTUNE

People who come to teach me a lesson whether I like it or not (also, flip that: people who come to learn a lesson from me, whether I'm aware I'm teaching it or not). If you are struggling with perceiving the truth of others and find that you overestimate or underestimate people's character, explore this planet's aspects.

SATURN

My guardians, who are the gods that visit Earth to check in on me but never let themselves be known. If you feel like time is not on your side, and things are not adding up deeply, explore all things happening with Saturn in your chart.

JUPITER

My teachers who do not know that they are my teachers and come completely from love. If you are struggling to find true mentors and teachers on your path, take time to connect with Jupiter and explore her aspects.

MARS

Those who come in regularly to my life on their terms, for whom I serve through the sacred dedication from my soul to share astrology. If you are struggling to get your conscious action taking to lead you to your goals, check in on your natal Mars and what's happening in relation to the other planets.

I have been working with orbits for years. I know where each person orbits in my world, and I'm hyperaware of how much information and time I share with people. The closer to me, the more you get. At those levels, it can be hard to understand me. I mean, how can *Emily* suffer from anxiety? There are contradictions in my field that do not make sense linearly and are very hard for someone to understand about me. I let that be okay. I place people in the right orbit in my universe.

Within the Water element, we seek to heal, retreat and restore. We need to create meaning and understanding around who we are and the work we do. We need boundaries. Boundaries are at first invisible and felt before you are able to communicate and enforce them.

The Water pillar is a point in the creative process of letting the invisible weight on your shoulders disappear and dissolve, because it's not real anyway.

When we grow without rest—we grow in strange ways. We grow, and we grow, and we grow, and then one day, we are shocked to see what we have turned into. There is an assumption that life took the wheel, but the truth is we lost control. We struggle to see where or how we lost control over our own path. Might I suggest that this is a wound deep within the collective? Might I suggest that in the failure to prioritize rest (both mental and physical), we are setting ourselves up for failure?

The heavier your energy feels, the more you need rest. The more you feel like life has gotten away from you or you will do that in five years, the more you need rest. The more you wander in circles and feel like you are repeating, the more you need rest. Whenever you complete a project, you need rest. And for all that is holy, when it is Mercury retrograde—you need rest.

After you complete your readings to gather your testimonials, you definitely need to prioritize some time of rest and disconnect. This means you can actively seek rest. You can plan for it and ensure that you receive it. So, what can you plan and schedule for yourself right now to ensure you do this? What is needed for you to rest?

For me, rest has been hard because I love creating. It feels difficult to unsuction myself to whatever it is I am up to. However, when I do pull myself away and force myself to lie in my hammock in the sun, it eventually begins to feel glorious and restorative. I used to rest only when I was physically exhausted or sick, and guess what? That did not serve me as a long-term solution.

If you rest only when you have to, you will always leak energy. Learning to rest in rhythm is how you avoid burnout, fuel your own light, and keep rising without falling. Make a promise to yourself that rest, healing, and restoration are equally important to all other steps in the creative process.

14
THE ROLES WE PLAY IN LIFE

In life, we play roles, and the zodiac personifies this dynamic. There isn't a single one-dimensional soul out there with only "Aries" in them. We are all the signs at varying degrees, and this is also why we desire to play various roles throughout our incarnation.

Roles we play are happening all around us. The "doctor" is a role just as much as the "actor." I have long been telling my children how grateful I am that I get to play "the role of Mother" to them in this life. I recognize that there is a choice and free will when it comes to our roles. This may not always have been so, but I believe it is true today.

One way that you can work with Water and consciously create these moments of rest is to embrace the roles you play and to acknowledge that you are, in fact, playing them. By doing this, you will allow your boundaries to harden, and the natural side effect is that you will be able to rest fully in between roles.

Over the years, I have gotten clear about what the role of playing an astrologer looks like in my life and what it means to me. Please keep in mind that we embrace the role so we can actively release it; we are doing this to align with the Water element, since it can be helpful to put roles on and take them off. There is a natural resting state right there in between, and that is a natural way to invite in more of the Water element.

Here are some beliefs I have chosen for my role as an astrologer:

BELIEF #1:
I'M PLAYING THE ROLE OF "ASTROLOGER" WHEN I AM IN MY SESSIONS.

When we actively define the "when," we are also defining the "when not." I desire to provide a powerful experience to my clients, but I also need realistic expectations of myself. I simply could not function if I had the responsibility of astrologer at all times. Those who take on that level within the role are often able to do this only by automating much of their process and outsourcing. I'm playing the role of astrologer only in sessions, and thus if someone desires for me to play that role in their life, they must hire me and respect that boundary I have placed.

BELIEF #2:
I'M RESPONSIBLE FOR CREATING MY SCHEDULE.

When you schedule your "shifts," you are able to designate time for your role. This is a powerful practice since it frees up and respects all the other roles you play. I try to keep two days a week available for my role as an astrologer, and when I'm not in that role, I'm doing other things. It feels refreshing and exciting for me since I don't always have on my "astrologer hat." When I do play my role, I feel grateful and honored to do it. It brings me energy.

BELIEF #3:
I DESERVE A BUFFER OF TIME TO PREPARE.

I do not feel that I play my role best when I am rushed and thrown into the session. This is due to my own energy and also the energy of a client "needing it now." I can 100 percent relate to wanting to get into a chart immediately, but I also hold my containers very steady to ensure my performance. In order to support my role, I have a forty-eight-hour buffer built into my scheduling system. If you try to book me, it prevents you from scheduling within that forty-eight-hour buffer. I find that this benefits my clients and me equally, by allowing us both to come to the meeting with the right mindset and emotional state.

BELIEF #4:
MY ROLE IS TO TRANSLATE AND INTERPRET.

I know we touched on this belief at the beginning of the book, but I can't stress this enough. The point of my role as an astrologer (as I chose to play it) is to interpret and translate astrology. I have no other strange ideas about who I am, what I'm capable of doing, or what my mission is here on Earth. I like translating and interpreting astrology for my clients, and by defining this objective, I release all the weight of having to be something I simply am not.

BELIEF #5:
MY ROLE IS TO TREAT EVERYONE THE SAME.

I like to remain consistent in my approach, personality, and demeanor within the context of my role as an astrologer. I do tend to become more soft when talking about sensitive topics, and a bit more rough when joking through the other comical human experiences we all share. Overall, I follow my outline each and every time, and I alter it on the basis of the client's needs. From this place of consistency within myself, I am better able to measure what is mine versus what is not. I know my role so well that I pull my energy into my field, and I don't get entangled with the person on the other side. It simply is an impossibility for me.

Water is about resting so we can let go of what no longer serves us. We are our own worst enemies, most of the time holding stagnant energy in our fields, wondering what is wrong. We hold on to things and wonder why we feel so heavy in this world. We have burdens within us from ten years ago that weigh us down, and this need not be our truth. Through rest, you find redemption. Through true rest, you are restored. Water heals, and yet, it also reveals.

Learning to embrace your role and to allow it to move into and out of you creates a sense of rest. I don't mentally worry about my clients during the week or my sessions. I do my work while I am in the work, and when I am out, I simply rest from that role.

15 WAYS TO NURTURE AND SUSTAIN YOUR SOUL

Most people think that sleep is enough, but I don't think it is the case, as I said in the previous chapter. If you go to bed but don't feel like you hit the "reset button," and you don't feel like you're starting your day with a clean slate, then you know it wasn't enough. We are overly driven most of the time (at least the people who wind up in my orbit). We are always working, trying, creating, moving, and doing, and this comes with very little time for rest and enjoying.

Sometimes I feel like my words can't properly describe what I am getting at, and this is a struggle for me as a writer. I say rest, but I don't mean to be completely still or unmoving, dead, or asleep. I mean rest in the sense that you disentangle, pull back, and give *life* back to *Life*.

Letting go is not a physical act but an emotional one. It is not impinging your emotional desires on any spiritual being, including yourself. It is the full presence and perhaps the meeting point of the active and passive states, the masculine and the feminine, the multidimensional and the linear.

For within this part of the creative process, the new ideas you seek live and are actively wanting to connect with you. BUT if you enter it to try to retrieve what you need to get what you want, it will slip through your hands and push you away. It will send you in circles, because you are disturbing its truth, and as far as I know, this state cannot be deceived.

Here is a list of ways that I believe will allow you to reach this watery place when approached with the right intentions in your heart:

GETTING INTO NATURE

Walks and hikes are a great way to connect and reach this state of rest within your soul. I don't mean hikes in the sense of climbing Everest, where it is some sort of ego achievement. Instead, I'm talking more about the regular places in your life where you can build in this connection so that it is easy and natural. Perhaps it's when you're walking your dog, and there is no real ego gratification in the process. Maybe it is sitting by a lake and drinking your morning coffee. Maybe it is watching the sunset from your porch swing and listening to the chimes sing. You find it is inconsequential, and you would never boost the experience because it is complete within itself. It fills you with stillness. My favorite nature spots are closest to my home.

MEDITATION

Stilling the body in an active posture can be a very powerful way to rest and let go, as long as you don't enter into meditation for egoic gains. Meditate to find ways to connect to *yourself* within *Yourself*. Listen to your voice, don't force it quiet. Meditation is about releasing control and letting things move through you. My favorite instruction on meditation is by Alan Watts.

PHYSICAL EXERCISE

There is an energy that one enters when running, swimming, or exercising. It isn't that they are thinking about how great their body will look, but rather that they are fully connected and internally reaching this state of watery rest or connection to nothingness. This is where the soul is being moved by the spirit, and they meet in that place. You will know you are there because it feels like you are doing the exercise for the connection inside without a yearning for that exercise to bring a connection on the outside. My favorite exercise is walking, and I do this daily.

HOBBIES WITHOUT PURPOSE

When you have a hobby that you do without a purpose, you will absolutely reach a watery place. It feels like you are just flowing through and being. It is very childlike and is not about proving anything or making money. Often, hobbies turn into our work, and thus they no longer create a resting state. My latest hobbies are rollerblading, tap dancing, and going on hiking adventures.

LISTENING TO MUSIC
THAT CALMS YOU

Music is a very powerful medicine on Earth, and I believe it to be single-handedly the greatest ally I have ever known. When music permeates my life, I feel a sort of ease in my being. Different types of music have different impacts on different people. My husband will listen to heavy metal, and it will have a transcendent and calming impact on him. I simply could never feel that way with that type of music, because it affects me differently. You must find music that brings you into a sort of resting state. For me, it is when the music feels like it is in my background or like it is the soundtrack for the experience I'm in.

You'll notice that intention has a lot to do with whether or not you will fully submerge yourself in Water. Writing to release and connect with yourself can do this, but writing copy for a website would not serve this same purpose. Going hiking on a date would be different than hiking by yourself. When you enter the Water essence without truly seeking to let go, you get spit right back out into Fire.

I think the elements are cyclical. Water does, in fact, lead back into Fire. And once you start to pay attention to this, you will see the irony. As we go to seek rest, we accidentally light ourselves back on Fire, often too soon and too frequently.

In the zodiac, the elemental pattern is repeated three times: Fire, Earth, Air, Water. The energy of Pisces leads into Aries, the energy of Cancer leads into Leo, and the energy of Scorpio leads into Sagittarius. Water always leads to Fire, and the goal is to not skip or move through the phase too fast! It's almost like there is suction energy that wants to pull us through, but we must resist and remind ourselves it is okay to let go.

16

SELF-COMPASSION MUST COME FIRST

Congratulations! You've done a profound amount of energy work and physical work throughout this book. As astrologers, we are here to marry the unseen with the seen. We connect the dots for people, share astrology in meaningful ways, and do work that is incredibly rewarding both for ourselves and the people we serve.

I want to share a paradigm shift that happened for me recently, and though it will seem inconsequential, small, and meaningless, I need you to know that it is not.

I was eating raisins and talking with my husband, and for some reason, we got on the subject of where the raisin comes from. I said something like, "I've never actually had a real raisin 'cause I eat only the dried version." And my husband replied, "Honey . . ."

In my mind, I always thought that dried raisins came from raisins. And then my husband laid it on me: "A dried raisin is, in fact, a grape."

I kid you not, I did not believe the man! I argued and fought! I said, "No way! Dried cranberries come from cranberries. Dried apricots come from apricots. Why in the world would they call them raisins and not dried grapes? A dried raisin has to be a raisin."

Unfortunately, my rationalizing ego was soon met with evidence to prove the truth: my husband pointed out the

picture of the grapes on the container. I laughed myself right back to heaven because I simply was so profoundly bewildered, and what a joy that I saw the beautiful innocence of my ego at that moment.

We are always learning.

I had a paradigm shift of the mind and the heart at the same time.

What I learned is that you are never dumb or stupid in the right company. You are never less than or worthless. And our ego is always going to have blind spots or hiccups. If you know and accept that you will forever be in a state where you have flaws or, as I like to call them, hiccups, you open your heart to compassion.

My husband and I laughed so hard because we have compassion for each other and ourselves. I also realized through that experience that another person might be ashamed of this blunder, and that makes my heart sad because this is how we start to shut ourselves out and create a disconnect from our souls. If we are not allowed to make mistakes with dignity, how can we possibly survive here on Earth?

My ego didn't do anything wrong, and it was very clever in its reasoning and had a lot to say! I mean, she had me fooled (and herself!) when she told me, "But dried cranberries are cranberries, and dried apricots are apricots! Correct? How can this be?"

I want you to have compassion for yourself as you grow. It really will be okay that you will make simple mistakes that you will make right along the way. We are humans, after all, and the learning curve always exists. Be love inside yourself, to yourself, and through yourself. If you can find compassion for yourself, it is such a very easy thing to extend to others.

What I've always loved and admired about astrology is its ability to make us think differently. I've never approached it thinking that the answers were inside a chart or that it was my job to tell people what to do. I definitely point out obvious windows of opportunity like "Jupiter transiting the seventh house for love every twelve years," but I trust that astrology does the work for me in ways that add up over time and in ways I could never really be aware of.

This is what our job is:

- To honor the connection created between the cosmos and Earth and to support others in seeing, embracing, and knowing that they are guided and loved. We are all made of the same "stuff."
- To take time to interpret the meaning of the placements and to have meaningful conversations that can open up the heart and the mind at the same time.
- To witness the hard work that the ego goes through in every life, and to have compassion for all people on Earth regardless of what we see.
- To remain an advocate of free will and to empower people to make decisions that they feel are right in their hearts.

With the Water element, we search for meaning. When we do this well, we don't force the creative process and jump straight back into Fire before we are ready. We find the mythical and very real place of flow. Not only are we led by the cosmic forces, but we feel them and embrace them inside ourselves. We know where we are, and we know where we are going. We are hugged by the repetition of the creative force: fire, earth, air, water.

Fire, earth, air, water.

Fire, earth, air, water.

Fire, earth, air, water.

And we are now complete with this current creative cycle.

AN INVITATION

Hello again, new astrologer
(who is not so *new* anymore)!

It is my passion to teach, train, coach, and develop astrologers. I love passing on this wisdom and seeing others succeed in their unique ways. I truly want to thank you for purchasing this book and allowing me to teach and share with you through the creative process of the astrological elements.

I struggled deeply with depression most of my early life. There was a sense that something was off and that I needed to figure out why I was here. I would look around, and no one in my life was asking these existential questions. My mind kept asking, "Why am I here?," "What is the purpose of this?," and "Why isn't anyone telling the truth?"

I felt like an outsider for much of my life. I took refuge in the metaphysical book section and the mystical books hidden in small crystals stores. I just knew there was more than people were telling me. When I found astrology, something clicked. Astrology gave me all I needed, because it was direct from the source and resonated as the truth vibration in my soul. The raw data that it provided me to work with was 100 percent truth, and I knew it. I felt it. I'm assuming you feel the same and love accessing this wisdom. I'm also assuming you want to empower others, that you want to be a cosmic consultant, not a gypsy hidden away at the fair.

If you desire to continue the journey with me, I highly recommend my first two workbooks, *Claiming Your Power through Astrology* and *Your Cosmic Compass*. Additionally, I have created an Astrologer Training Program that is available on my website www.absolutelyastrology.com that will go over the planets, signs, houses, aspects, and more.

Your teacher,

Emily

(Capricorn Rising, Taurus Sun, Taurus Moon)